INFORMATION TECHNOLOGY IN 21ST CENTURY

INFORMATION TECHNOLOGY IN 21ST CENTURY

(In 9 Volumes)

CYBERSPACE AS PUBLIC DOMAIN

The Role of Civil Society

(Volume 2)

PROF. RAMESH CHANDRA

Vice-Chancellor, Bundelkhand University, Jhansi (U.P.)

Publication

KALPAZ PUBLICATIONS

DELHI–110052

INFORMATION TECHNOLOGY IN 21ST CENTURY
Cyberspace as Public Domain: The Role of Civil Society
(Information Technolgy)

Rs. 8000 (Set)
Rs. 900 (each volume)

ISBN: 81-7835-158-7 (Set)
ISBN: 81-7835-160-9 (Vol. 2)

Published in 2003 in India by
Kalpaz Publications
C-30, Satyawati Nagar
Delhi-110052
E-mail: kalpaz@hotmail.com

Laser Typesetting at: A.S. Printers
Printed at: Chawla Offset Printers, Delhi

Preface

Technology is a cold and neutral medium. It is people, individuals that bring passion, life and meaning to this medium. It somehow seems that this point is missed as society collectively races to embrace technology. We are the inheritors of our past that we did not bring about but the creators of our collective futures. At this point in our history we have a collective responsibility as to how our society will shape itself. We have the capacity to create change in our societies through speaking out. Many changes do occur in society when people speak out and spark debate. It is now time for such a discourse over the future of technology. We need to develop a philosophical base about all these new technologies so society drives technology and not technology drives us.

The network-centered information society is just starting to evolve. Information and knowledge are forming one of the basic ingredients of such society. However, if that information and knowledge does not permeate the texture of the global society and be assimilated by the different societies worldwide, it will have limited impact on the global community. Cyberspace is creating a global platform where a worldwide forum is evolving that is becoming vital to economic, social and political success.

This book deals with many facts of society as public domain. It describes the move towards online activism, and the use of the internet as an information and communications tool to forward common social goals. It looks at the distinctions between electronic governance and electronic democracy and how the latter is having a wide impact on civil society. For administrators, managers, information technologists, analysts, students and anyone in the field of information and communication technologies, this book is destined to become one of the most frequently consulted references.

Editor

Contents

1

Introduction

There is an abundance of utopian scenarios available that promise sustainable development once digital highways have been constructed. In such perspectives the deployment of new information and communication technologies (ICTs) ushers in a "new civilization", an "information revolution", or a "knowledge society". This line of thought emphasizes historical discontinuity as a major consequence of technological developments.

New social values will evolve, new social relations will develop, the "zero sum society" comes to a definite end, once ICTs have realized worldwide access for all to information. The current highway utopias forecast radical changes in economics, politics and culture. In the economy the ICTs will create more productivity and improved chances for employment. They will upgrade the quality of work in many occupations. They will also offer myriad opportunities for small-scale, independent and decentralized forms of production. In the domain of politics, the decentralized and increase access to unprecedented volumes of information will improve the process of democratisation. All people will be empowered to participate in public decision making. In the cultural domain, new and creative lifestyles will emerge as well as vastly extended opportunities for different cultures to meet and understand each other, new virtual communities will be created that easily cross across all the traditional borderlines of age, gender, race, and religion.

The essential vehicle to make these dreams come true will be the project of a "Global Information Infrastructure" (GII). The GII was launched by the US Vice President Al Gore in a 1994 speech at the conference of the International Telecommunication Union in Buenos Aires.

The proposal has received a good deal of international political and corporate support. The meeting of the G-7 in Brussels in February 1995 decided to definitely move ahead with the implementation of this global infrastructure. The G-7 Final Declaration stated that the global information society is expected to enrich people worldwide by providing to developing countries and countries in transition the chance "to leapfrog stages of technology".

Several countries such as Canada, Japan, Singapore, and the European Union are intent on the rapid realisation of national information infrastructures in the near future. Also the developing world has shown considerable interest. The African region provides a good illustration. The interest in ICTs was very prominent during the First African Regional Symposium on Telematics for Development (1995) and also at the 21st session of the Conference of African Ministers responsible for Economic, Social and Development

Planning (1995). Also in 1995 the Workshop on the Role and Impact of Information and Communication Technologies in Development (held at Cairo, Egypt) recommended that "without proper national information and communication policies, strategies and implementation plans, countries will not be able to partake fully in the global information society".

Although most African countries are not known as hot spots for ICT development, the United Nations Economic Commission for Africa Conference of Ministers adopted on May 2, 1995 Resolution 795 (XXX), "Building Africa's Information Highway". African ministers for economic and social development requested in the resolution that the ECA sets up a high-level working group on information and communication technologies in Africa made up of African technical experts with a view to preparing a plan of action in this field.

The High-Level Working Group (after meetings in Cairo, Addis Ababa and Dakar) produced Africa's Information Society Initiative: An Action Framework to Build Africa's Information and Communications Infrastructure. In early May 1996 the plan was authorized for implementation by the Conference of Ministers meeting at Addis Ababa.

The Conference on Information Society and Development (ISAD) in South Africa, May 1996, was the venue for the launching of the African Information Society initiative. By 2010 this initiative foresees for Africa an information society in which: "Every man and woman, schoolchild, village, government office, and business can access information through computers and telecommunications; Information and decision support systems are used to support decision making in all the major sectors of each nation's economy; Access is available throughout the region to international, regional and national information highways; A vibrant private sector exhibits strong leadership in growing information-based economies; African information resources are accessible globally reflecting content on tourism, trade, education, culture, energy, health, transport, and natural-resource management; and Information and knowledge empower all sectors of society".

Today -increasingly - also big info-communications business is taking a growing interest. Companies such as Time/Warner are making massive investments to secure a profitable place on the Information Superhighway.

The Global Information Infrastructure project has a large number of computopian prophets such as European Commissioner Martin Bangemann, the CEOs of companies such as AT&T, IBM, Microsoft and American Express, mediatycoon Rupert Murdoch, authors such as Alvin Toffler and US Vice President Al Gore.

The latter stated in his Buenos Aires address that the Global Information Infrastructure is the essential prerequisite to sustainable development. It will provide solutions to environmental problems, improve education and health care, create a global marketplace and forge a new Athenian age of democracy.

It is obviously true that ICTs can perform tasks that are indeed essential to democratic and sustainable social development. They can provide low-cost, high speed, worldwide interactive communications among large numbers of people, unprecedented access to information sources, alternative channels for information provision that counter the commercial news channels, and they can support networking, lobbying, and mobilizing.

The Fourth World Conference on Women in Beijing (1995), for example, showed the benefits that women's groups could get out of the use of ICTs. The general experience of the women's groups involved in the Beijing electronic networking (despite all the real limitations) was that the low cost and high speed communications had improved organisational efficiency and had facilitated access to up-to-date information. NGOs in the South indicated that the networks had allowed them to influence the conference agenda, to mobilise lobbies, and to counter commercial press coverage. The participants generally felt the technology had strong empowerment potential.

There are however serious obstacles in the way of realising the empowerment potential of ICTs.

Economic factors: The introduction and use of ICTs does not take place in a social vacuum. This process cannot be separated from the emerging global communication order. The reality of this order is a global info- communications market that yields in 1997 over 1.5 trillion dollar in revenues and that continues to feature a process of Mergers and Acquisitions which most likely leads to the control of the world's information and cultural supply by some four to six multimedia megaconglomerates around the turn of the century.

Today's forerunner of the projected Global Information Infrastructure, the Internet has begun to attract the attention of the major forces in this global market place. The Internet -at present a public meeting place where more than 30 million PC users in some 150 countries exchange information, search databases, play games and chat- and that has been guided by the rule of sharing information for free, has now been discovered as a major vehicle for commercial advertising. This raises the question whether the Internet will remain an open, free, competitive, egalitarian public space? This is highly unlikely since the Net does not develop outside the current global economic order.

The Net is moving fast toward developing into the new global advertising medium. There is a great battle going on with at stake the future control of the world's largest network. Moneymaking on the Net will require to turn it into an advertising medium. In order for companies to re-coup their enormous investments, advertising and sales will be essential. The competition to attract advertising dollars is already on its way. As a result, a communicative structure that so far has been public, non-commercial, non-regulated, non-censored, anarchistic and very pluralistic may soon turn into a global electronic shopping mall.

It is difficult to understand how the current transformation of the Net from a public forum into a commercial vehicle (much the way this happened in many countries with television) can contribute to the realisation of the empowerment potential of ICTs. In any case, if the Global Information Infrastructure project is predominantly driven by the search for profits, there is little probability that current inequalities in access and use of ICTs will go away.

Political obstacles: An important political obstacle to the creation of open, public networks is the current trend towards deregulatory policies around the world. Their bottom-line is that the introduction and use of ICTs should predominantly if not totally be a matter of market relations. The G-7 and the EU governments have made it repeatedly understood that the GII will have to be constructed primarily through private investments. Global and regional policy making addresses primarily the removal of all obstacles that might stand in the way of the unhindered operation of the major ICT-investors on markets around the world.

The policies of WTO and IMF are instrumental to supporting the global commercial media system. They are not particularly helpful to the democratisation of the world's info-com sector. A landmark in deregulatory policies is the WTO telecom agreement of early 1997. The agreement requires signatory countries (68 countries that represent 98% of the $600 billion telecom trade) to liberalise their markets to foreign competition. According to various governments this will strongly facilitate the global Superhighway, but most likely as an infrastructure for transnational business, not necessarily as platform for public debate on social development.

The agreement has seriously compromised the chances for universal network access as national policies may be considered anti-competitive if governments intervene in the market to guarantee universal service. According to industry spokesmen the agreement will speed up the search for global alliances.

Info-telecom disparity: There seems general agreement in the scientific literature and in public policy statements that the gap in access to ICTs between the developed and developing countries is widening and that this hinders the integration of all countries into the Global Information Society. The seriousness of the gap is clearly demonstrated by the figures of the world distribution of telephony. There are 1 billion telephones in the world and approximately 5.7 billion people. Today for some 15% of the world population there is some 71% of the world's main telephone lines. Low income countries (where 55% of the world population lives) have less than 5% of the world share of telephone lines. High income countries have 50 telephone lines per 100 inhabitants.

Many low income countries have less than one telephone line per 100; this ranges from Cambodia with 0.06 to China with 0.98 in 1992 (according to figures provided by the ITU/BDT Telecommunication Indicator Database). More than 50% of the world's people have never even used a telephone! Less than 6% of Internet computers are in Eastern Europe, Asia, Africa, the Middle East and Latin America. Less than 4% of WWW users are found in the Third World. In India there is 1 telephone line and 0,2 PC for 100 people, this compares to 49 lines and 15 PCs in Japan, and 63 lines and 21 PCs per 100 people in the USA.

The reality of the widening gap in ICT capacity raises the serious concern that the poorer countries may not be able to overcome the financial and technical obstacles that hamper their access to the new technologies.

An obvious question regarding the financial obstacles is whether the international community is ready to provide the massive investments needed for the renovation, upgrading and expansion of networks in developing countries. By way of illustration of the scope of funds involved: it would take some US $ 12 billion to get 50% of the Philippine population on the Internet. To increase teledensity from 0.46 lines per 100 inhabitants to 1 per 100 in Sub-Saharan Africa would require an investment of US$ 8 billion. A particular funding problem also arises if the current Internet has to be transformed into a global interactive electronic highway.

This demands a radical expansion of current bandwidth to transport all these signals. If one was to provide broadband capacity to all US citizens, it would demand investments of several hundreds of billions dollars.

In response to the challenge of the info-telecom gap many public and private donor institutions have proposed plans for the elimination of the disparity. The concern about the gap has inspired The World Bank for example, established early 1995 the Information for Development Program with the brief to assist developing countries with their integration into the global information economy.

The ITU has in 1995 established WorldTel -an ambitious project to generate private investments to bridge the telecom gap in the world by developing basic infrastructures. WorldTel aims at some 40 million telephone connections in developing countries in the next ten years. It aims at an investment fund of minimal one billion dollar. AT&T plans that its Africa One project will have a fully operational optical fibre cable around the whole continent of Africa by 1999 to provide connections for all the major coastal cities.

Also Siemens and Alcatel have designs (Afrilink and Atlantis-2 respectively) to provide telecom connections, especially to West Africa. Both the International Satellite Organization (IntelSat) and theRegional African Satellite Organisation are actively promoting the expansion of e-mail services for the continent.

Apart from the problem that all these plans do not match the funds that are really required, they also raise the critical issue of the appropriateness of the technologies transferred and the capacity of the recipient countries to master them. The present discussion on the gap provides no convincing argument that the technology owners will change their attitudes and policies towards the international transfer of technology. Throughout the past decades the prevailing international policies on transfer of technology have erected formidable obstacles to the reduction of North-South technology gaps. To-day, there is no indication that the current restrictive business practices, the constraints on the ownership of knowledge, and the rules on intellectual property rights that are adverse to developing country interests are radically changing.

There are presently no realistic prospects that the relations between ICT-rich and ICT- poor countries will change in the near future. The key actors in international ICT-policy making have expressed a clear preference to leave the construction of the Global Information Society to "the forces of the free market", and would seem that under the institutional arrangements of a corporate-capitalist market economy, the development of an equitable information society remains a very unlikely proposition. At any rate, it deserves to be questioned whether within the realities of the international economic order, there can be any serious reduction of the disparity. It may well be an illusion to think that ICT-poor countries could catch up or keep pace with the advancements in the northern countries. In the North the rate of technological development is very high and is supported by considerable resources. This is not to say that poor countries should not try to upgrade their Its. They should however not do this in the unrealistic expectation that those are ahead will wait for them. As a result, the situation may improve for the poorer countries, but the disparity will not go away.

The most immediate political challenge today is the insight that the use of ICTs for sustainable development will not be determined by technology but by politics. The realisation of their potential requires a re-thinking the wisdom of current deregulatory policies, a re-thinking of the role of public funding and a massive effort in training and education for the mastery of ICTs. This political agenda is unlikely to be seriously treated if ICT-policies are left to Princes and the Merchants alone. If market-driven arrangements are for some time to come- the standard environment in which ICTs will be deployed, then the only force that could make a real difference are the ordinary people who buy on the market and who have the (often unused and rarely recognised) power to say "no".

The realisation of the empowerment potential of ICTs should therefore primarily be the concern of civil society organisations. They need to mobilise and lobby for and with the ordinary men and women whose lives will be affected by the digital futures that are presently designed. To-day there is only a very modest beginning of a global civil activism in the info-communications sector through such organizations as the worldwide community radio association, AMARC, the Cultural Environment Movement and the People's Communication Charter. It is urgent that these movements begin to extend their reach by attracting the support of large public interest organisations (labour unions, educational institutions, religious bodies) and intergovernmental organisations such as UNESCO and ITU.

Since our cultural environment is as essential to our common future as the natural ecology, it is time that people's movements should focus on the organisation and quality of the production and distribution of information and other cultural expressions.

Mobilising the users community and stimulating critical reflection on the quality of the cultural environment is a tall order. However, it can be done and it is actually being done. There is an increasing number of individuals and groups around the world that begins to express concern about the quality of media performance. Also a beginning has been with the creation of a broad international movement of alert and demanding media users. The movement is based upon what has been called the People's Communication Charter.

The People's Communication Charter is an initiative of the Third World Network (Penang, Malaysia), the Centre for Communication & Human Rights (Amsterdam, the Netherlands), the Cultural Environment Movement (USA), and the AMARC-World Association of Community Radio Broadcasters (Peru/Canada).

In the early 1990s the academics and activists associated with the Third World Network in Penang and its affiliated Consumers Association of Penang initiated a debate on the feasibility of a world people's movement in the field of communication and culture.

The TWN and CAP had by then already an impressive record with the development of people's movements in such areas as international trade and the tropical rain forest. They had proved capable of bringing the concerns of grass roots people in Third World countries to the diplomatic negotiations of the Uruguay GATT multilateral trade round and the UNCED in Rio de Janeiro.

An obvious problem turned out to be that information consumers are not normally organised in representative associations. They are a diverse community, geographically dispersed and ideologically fragmented. In order to create a constituency for concerns about the quality of the cultural environment, the People's Communication Charter was initiated as a first step. This Charter provides the common framework for all those who share the belief that people should be active and critical participants in their social reality and capable of governing themselves. The People's Communication Charter can be a first step in the development of a permanent movement concerned with the quality of our cultural environment.

One of the ideas that has been launched for this implementation is to organise an International Tribunal that would receive complaints by signatories of the Charter and invite the parties involved to submit evidence and defense upon which the Tribunal could come to a judgement.

The Charter is not an end in itself. It provides the basis for a permanent critical reflection on those worldwide trends that determine the quality of our lives in the third millennium. It is therefore important to see the Charter as an open document that can always be updated, amended, improved, and expanded.

A very important moment in the PCC history was the Founding Convention of the Cultural Environment Movement when the first public ratification of the text took place. Recently, in June 1997, the governing body of the World Association for Christian Communication has endorsed the Charter. This was the conclusion of much discussion of the Charter by WACC members in its eight regions. The WACC Central Committee also proposed some important amendments to the text. Next year the Charter will be on the agenda of the General Assembly of AMARC and of the Paris Convention of the Cultural Environment Movement in April. For the United Nations celebration of the 50th anniversary of the Universal Declaration of Human Rights initiatives are being developed to secure some form of acclaim for the Charter from the international political community.

Most importantly, however, is at present to solicit more support for the ideas that the Charter embodies from individuals and institutions worldwide. In August 1996, for example, the Charter was displayed at the famous Dokumenta exhibition at Kassel, Germany. The text was discussed and signed by many visitors. The Web site of the Charter is the place where such events and the progress in widening support for the PCC is made public.

Beyond the text itself and its endorsement, the most critical element for the Charter's future is obviously its implementation. In an open, democratic, people's movement this cannot be organised by some central governing body. Implementation is very much the concern of local and national groups, either newly formed or already established for other (or similar) purposes.

The realisation of the people's right to communicate cannot be a homogeneous project. This will take different forms in different socio-cultural and political contexts. In one country this may be the institution of an Ombudsman office for the quality of the cultural environment, in another country a national prize may be awarded for the TV programme people find most in violation of the Charter's principles, in some place a civil society campaign to rescue public broadcasting may be necessary, somewhere else the focus may on the protection of children or the defense of the media interests of people with a handicap. This is really the business of ordinary people. It is also the ultimate test case for the meaning of the Charter. It only makes sense if eventually people themselves begin to be concerned about its implementation.

2

Information Transition

We are witnessing a phenomenal abundance of change in societies around the world in a very short period. The source of most of this change is new technologies and the Internet. In the past decade we have seen every aspect of the lives of individuals and organizations go through many evolutions and uncertainties. Large, medium and small corporations alike have discovered the need to adapt to the new technologies, or sink in the emerging global knowledge economy. There is no facet of life in the industrialized world that has not undergone some form of shift. The resultant new information economy has brought with it different approaches to work. There has been a surge in tele-workers, entrepreneurs and home run businesses. Corporations have downsized and knowledge workers migrate from company to company, open to the highest bidder and the organization with the best deal. The highly proficient, intelligent and innovative knowledge worker is in demand. Knowledge itself seems to have become a commodity in the marketplace of ideas. The pace of change has been so dizzying to some they have difficulty in meeting the challenges these shifts have brought. We now live in an information intense driven society.

Nowhere has this been more evident than with government, who are constantly having to cope with the persistently emerging new technologies and demands from citizens. In today's wired world, the interactive citizen is one of the fundamental cornerstones of change. The Internet has put new power into the hands of the citizen. Governments can no longer simply be dispensers of information, even in sophisticated forms being developed by many governments. But governments have not been passive observers and are rising to many of the challenges. New technologies are being used not only to deliver services to the public but also to enhance government administration and facilitate businesses.

This section looks at the means by which some governments are moving to electronic governance and what role information will play in the future. In this context, governance can be seen as both a means of using new technologies to deliver services to the citizen, and ways in which to change and improve the efficient methods of administration within governments themselves

Impact of the internet

At this stage of development few governments have effectively been able to involve their citizenry electronically in the democratic process. Many governments have been effective dispensers of information, which often passes as a means of enhancing the democratic process. There are many government initiatives seeking to help citizens to get online, seek feedback on government reports online, and develop listservs and discussion groups to elicit the views of the citizens. There are also many groups actively participating in online activities in the hope of influencing government policies. But for the most part, governments are far behind the activities of citizens online around the world. Those actively engaged in online activities involving social or political change see the Internet as a medium to foster, enhance and change the way people have traditionally engaged in the democratic process.

The story of the Internet and electronic democracy is a cautionary tale. Much of the enthusiasm and hope for new forms of democracy and citizen input into public issues, sound very like the gushing optimism expressed about the potential of television in its nascent years. It is not yet known if the potentials offered by the Internet will be met. Will the Internet become like television, an arid desert with only a small oasis of excellence? This is an important question because the potential is there for the Internet to become dominated by a few large, corporate interests, or subsumed by government regulation that could inhibit the freedoms offered by this new technology. There is also the danger in a recent trend indicating that people are increasingly spending more time in isolation sitting in front of their computer terminals.

A recent survey of 4,113 adults conducted by Stanford University's Institute for the Quantitative Study of Social Sciences found that "55 percent of Americans have access to the Internet at work or at home, and approximately 20 percent of regular Internet users spend more than 5 hours a week online. Of those 20 percent, 13 percent spend less time with family and friends, 8 percent attend fewer social events, and 25 percent spend more time working at home in addition to spending a full day at the office.

The findings of the study also support the assertion that Americans are abandoning traditional forms of mass media, such as newspapers and television, in favor of the Internet." There is wide potential of change here for the way people will interact as a society as the Internet continues to grow.

Suffice to say at the moment the Internet is creating major change both positive and negative. One of these changes is in the ways citizens are engaging in the democratic process and beginning to slowly altering the face of democracy. The next section looks at some of the initiatives and the reshaping of the face of democracy which online citizen participation is bringing.

Information as a democratic tool

This could well be the anthem for all those netizens who want to continue to recognize their particular identities on a medium that is increasingly being dominated by the corporate world. "We are the Internet" could well be the clarion call stating loudly and clearly that this medium is for all the people, that this is the medium, which will bring new forms of expression of the democratic will of the people.

However, "we are the Internet" is taking on a more prosaic meaning in that the growing connectivity with many forms of media is making all users of the Internet increasingly one with technology.

Within the next decade, or sooner, we will probably not even use the word the Internet, or the Net, because the actual convergences of technologies is creating a new phenomenon. Now an individual can be connected to the online world through a variety of technologies. In experimental stage in the labs now are glasses you will wear that will bring the online world to your lenses. You wont need to boot up and go through all the messy program commands as these glasses will be linked to a micro cellular device which will be voice activated. You will just say what you want, get your email, send a message, take a virtual tour of the office, meet others in virtual meeting spaces, go there anonymously with created identities, book a holiday, look for new online or whatever any of the things you want to do. You will be in cyberspace, disconnected from the physical offline world except for the glasses you are wearing.

Experiments are currently ongoing to have automated automobiles on the highways so all you have to do is program your destination (probably by voice) and off you go. The car, as it travels, will not necessarily go to the route you (once known as the driver) will tell it, as it is will be connected to a GPS (GeoPositioning Satellite) which will alert your autocar to any potential traffic jams or road problems ahead. Thus, your car (or, that is to say, the machine the technological masters are letting you occupy) will be diverted as needed to the most desirable and quickest5 route. This mapping of cars is not a fantasy or possible scenario for the future but a reality, as mapping programs already exist to get you to your destination by the quickest route. In much of the industrialised world most countries are already mapped electronically, thanks to satellite technology, and available on the Internet. Other ideas for the Internet include the wired home in which everything from your electricity to your heat to your refrigerator would be connected to the Internet and connected to whatever company is providing you with the service. Thus, the electricity corporation can adjust uses of electricity and your refrigerator can alert you when you are low on milk or, more probable still, send a message to your grocery supplier to send more supplies to you. This is all very efficient, and perhaps even a time server for the consumer, but do we want our lives to be governed by disparate pieces of technology? For the sake of efficiency and time do we really all want to be wired to a seamless technological mosaic? But this is just one small example of the technological world we are building.

That is not to say there are not intrinsic values to the Internet and the new technologies and that many have benefited. The Internet has been a tool of enrichment for large numbers of our populations. It has allowed diversity, the rise of the entrepreneur, the mushrooming of home businesses, the bringing together of family and friends through instant communications, the Internet has been a voice for many who for too long did not have the means to express themselves because prior mediums of the expression of communication have been controlled by the few. The Internet has been many things to many people. New, advanced medical technologies and scientific breakthroughs have lengthened our average life span and brought us better health and lifestyles.

On the Internet, there are pockets of dissent and discourse. there are many who use the new technologies for learning, to facilitate their businesses, to get a service, whether from government or business, play games with each other over long distances, keep in contact through email and a thousand and other good usages that can benefit the individual. We know the benefits, we know of the attempts of many professionals who seek to use the Internet to both gain knowledge and dispense and share knowledge. Perhaps, the most important feature of the Internet is that it has allowed individuals to communicate in ways not available before. This is an important new channel through which communication, ideas and knowledge can flow. The Smithsonian Institute in the United States, the British Library along with a wider consortium of universities and libraries are joining together to put online the Magna Carta, the Lindisfrane gospels and the entire contents of the Smithsonian online. Their purpose is to take the massive volumes of knowledge available in off line libraries and to make available online for the whole` world to benefit. The intent is simple: what an individual can get by going to a library should be available to the world through the Internet. But as with all things in life there are positive benefits and negative impacts. The questions now we must ask ourselves collectively are: how do we manage to grow the benefits while neutralizing many of the negative elements? And there are many negatives surfacing as technological advances far outstrips society's ability to determine the direction we will go as a result of the developments.

Technology is the modern spider that has increasingly built a web around our lives. The collective question for us as a society is: are we the fly now captured in this complex, intricate web or are we still the masters of our destiny? Where is the debate, discussions about the social, cultural and political impacts of technologies on our lives and what these technological changes are doing to our humanity? Has society become the fly willingly ensnared in this new web (and not simply the Web on the Internet) actually created by a few and used to drive the new economy and the engine of consumerism? Has electronic commerce and the burgeoning global information economy so subsumed the agendas of world governments that we can no longer objectively look at where we should be going? It can be persuasively argued that throughout history all new technologies have changed the way the world lives and operates as a society. Transportation brought the world together and television resulted in the global village that brought all of us on the planet closer together as a people (though not necessarily in a harmonious way). Now tourism is the world's second largest industry with millions of people on the move all around the world, experiencing and sharing in other cultures.

Of course, these millions are mostly from the rich nations. It appears we see nothing wrong in going to exotic and culturally challenging parts of the world, in the quest for something new and exciting and the next best thing to experience, and then pay scant attention to the many more millions of poor. Ironically, many will argue that tourism brings needed dollars and helps these economies. But even this does not ring with the hallowed sound of truth as studies show that those who benefit most are the western multinational recreational chains and others who sell their wares globally to all and sundry. Usually, the locals benefit only to the extent they receive minimum wages.

The point here is not a quick analysis of the rich vs. the poor but rather that we as a people who experience the offline world as we do, and are often blinded to the consequences, might be just as blinded to what technology is doing to us. The message might also be that most people don't really care and are happy to carry on enjoying the new wealth and comfort that technologies are bringing.

Whatever the opinions or views of individuals and governments in society it is evident that we need a far deeper debate and discourse over the impacts of technologies. There are concerns over ensuring all citizens have universal access to the Internet (and are free to use it or not use it as they wish), there are serious, abiding anxieties about the digital divide that is occurring throughout the world. Privacy laws, to protect people's information and endow on their certain rights over their own personal information, are spreading. But the implementation of such laws is but one small step. Articulation of these issues is just the start. We need deeper discourse. Ironically, it is this medium that affords the opportunity to bring such discourse forward.

This is why online e-Democracy is so important as this activity represents the power of this technology and how it can be used to embrace democracy and involve people in the social, economic, cultural and political issues of the day. This is a tool that can give people, the individual citizen, the power to influence public policy. Governments are slowly coming to realize that there is an undercurrent of democratic change going on in the world. The face of democracy is beginning to change and a few thousand at the moment are doing it. But this is a change that has the potential for growth.

Technology is a cold and neutral medium. It is people, individuals that bring passion, life and meaning to this medium. It somehow seems that this point is missed as society collectively races to embrace technology. We are the inheritors of our past that we did not bring about but the creators of our collective futures.

At this point in our history we have a collective responsibility as to how our society will shape itself. We have the capacity to create change in our societies through speaking out.

Many changes do occur in society when people speak out and spark debate. It is now time for such a discourse over the future of technology. We need to develop a philosophical base about all these new technologies so society drives technology and not technology drives us.

This next section looks at the distinctions between electronic governance and electronic democracy and how the latter is having a wide impact on civil society. The move towards online activism, and the use of the Internet as an information and communications tool to forward common social goals, is important to understand. The mechanisms evolving in the developed world to influence government policy can also be used as tools to help those in the developing world.

Electronic democracy

Many governments are moving to electronic governance. In this context governance can be seen as both a means to using new technologies to deliver services to the citizen and ways in which to change and improve the efficient methods of administration within governments themselves. Another element looked at in this section is the means as whereby governments will increasingly be able to involve citizens in the democratic process of government.

At this stage of development few governments have effectively been able to involve their citizenry electronically in the democratic process. For the most part, governments are far behind the activities of citizens online around the world, who see the Internet as a medium to foster, enhance and change the way people have traditionally engaged in the democratic process. There are some efforts on different government fronts.

In the United States and Great Britain governments are looking at setting up online voting. The British Electoral Commission recently announced that they would be looking into the feasibility of online voting.

A similar announcement was made in California in January 2000. February 28, 2000 saw the meeting of the first Internet Voting Technology Alliance in Washington, D.C. Initial participants included: Safevote, of San Rafael, Calif.; VoteHere, of Kirkland, Wash.; Modulo Security Solutions, of Rio de Janeiro; International Foundation for Election Systems, of Washington, D.C., and e-Elections, of Oakland, Calif.

The group met to get public funding for their activities. The group's goal will be, amongst other things, to develop the proper tools and protocols to ensure online voting is safe and secure for the citizen and is not subject to corruption or manipulation.

But this is a tool for voting under the current system of democracy as we know it. People were able to participate online in this opening assembly at Governments, for the most part, are far behind the public in developing tools for electronic democracy. There are some good initiatives, such as the web sites of the British Prime Minister, which seek to garner public comment, opinion and discussion. There was also an online consultation run by the British parliamentary Select Committee on Public Administration.

It was run from mid-November 1999 for one month, in connection with their inquiry into e-democracy and e-government. The online discussion centred on "innovations in citizen participation in government". The Committee sent out electronic notices, which were picked up around the world, asking people to send in their experiences in e-democracy and e-governance.

These are true, but limited, steps towards electronic democracy. However, on the whole, governments tend simply to provide information on their web sites and use the Internet, and other technologies, to deliver services electronically.

The prime example of this is the US White House site which is primarily an information tool and conduit to executive agency web sites. It was only in January 2000 that President Clinton announced that government had to be interactive with the citizen.

The dispensing of information, without substantial input from the citizen, is not a real interactive transaction. Yet, the Internet in and of itself is an interactive medium. Individuals on the Internet understand this and, for growing legions of people, it is becoming a force that is changing the nature of democracy as we know it today...

But this is just part of the wider picture of developments in electronic democracy. In fact, individuals and groups are coming together online around the world to influence policy.

Politicians are also using the web. In the United States every Presidential candidate has a web site. There are also alternative web sites by interested citizens or groups who want to have their say about the candidates.

There are also other groups who are offering sites which will present in-depth analysis of the issues in the upcoming presidential and congressional elections as well as elections at the local and state level.

The online world of democratic activism is growing around the world. This section looks at the emerging trends in electronic democracy, how citizens active online are changing the nature of democracy as we have understood it, and how governments are going to have to tap into this emerging trend.

In the wired world, the online citizen is increasingly playing more and more of a role in the democratic process. There are now hundreds of groups involved, from the community and local level to the national and international stage, in some way working to have an influence on government policies and programs, and on societal issues of our age. Because of these changes, the process of government will soon no longer be controlled from the top and micro-managed by a few when it comes to public policy. In the changing wired world, citizens are voicing their say.

Governments may not necessarily be listening, but the thousands upon thousands of people engaging in discourse on the thousand and one issues of the day are certainly listening to each other. This is resulting in powerful currents of change which are only beginning to manifest themselves. Electronic democracy is not about citizens voting on a multitude of referendums as laid out by governments. Electronic democracy is citizens engaging in the political process in means chosen by individuals.

E-Commerce currently dominates the mass media as the main phenomenon of the Internet. But the real story lies in the changes being brought by the thousands of groups and people online around the world, who are engaged in some sort of civic activism, political engagement, or just plain discourse and debate, on the issues that are important to them.

The most evident manifestation of this was in Seattle in December 1999,subsequent events at the IMF and World Bank meetings in Washington, D.C. in March, 2000 and the meetings in Prague in September, 2000.

The massive protests in Seattle, Washington, D.C. and Prague over the rise of corporate elitism and globalisation on the agendas of governments, demonstrated the power of the Internet in bringing people out to express their demands to be part of the process. These people were determined to have their say. Not only did they express their beliefs and ideas but governments were forced to listen.

There is some growing awareness in government that their old dynamics of secrecy, closed meetings, and invitations to the special few to be part of the process, are starting to fade. In Seattle we saw the first shot fired across the bow of the old world order of democracy as we have known it.

What we are witnessing is an emergence from the traditional forms of representative democracy to a new form that has yet to be given a name. For the moment, we can call it cyberism, as an expression of a particular form of politics. But that is still an expression born out of the old paradigm. The new democracy we see surfacing is more the expression of individual voices that congeal into a collective whole over ideas that the society of peoples online develop into a consensus. And while a consensus might be formed on major issues, people are still in a position to express their individual thoughts and ideas (even if they range from the erudite to the opinionated). In this emerging world we see the evolution of a true populist democracy.

Although people's ideas do not necessarily have to be acted upon individually, the means exist for individuals to communicate freely to an audience. That audience can be large or small, but it represents a freedom for the individual that has not existed up to this point in time. The mass media still hold the reigns of mass communication. It is still important to get that letter to the editor published so you can reach a wide readership. But with this new medium of the Internet you can write something and it will reach the level of interest in the audience out there.

In Seattle, Washington, D.C. and Prague, the initial protests were organized off line and online. And it was the Internet that gave this movement the international momentum to make it the effective demonstration, and the somewhat collective voice of outsiders, that it became. It was the clarion call for democracy from voices across the world. It has become the symbol not only for the voices able to speak from the Internet, but of the fact that the citizenry has found the ideal tool by which they can bypass all the normal channels of government. This is not a small development at this stage in our history.

Many people talk about the "Individual" being in control, or having great power because of the ability to tap into the world through the keyboard, but it is not certain if the real power is understood. It has mostly been identified as the power of the consumer to buy the product he wants, or read the online newspaper of choice. In fact, what has actually happened is we have collectively opened a Pandora's box. And it really is too early to state exactly all the changes that will occur. It can be said with certainty that there is a powerful current of knowledge and ideas now circulating the world.

What once took months or years to turn into an issue now can occur in less than a day. This is the true power of the citizen. This is the story of the evolution of a truly populist democracy, an emerging democracy in which issues are being transformed from the hands of the few elite to thousands (and one day will be millions).

It is like throwing one seed into the garden and from it a flower grows. Throw the seed of an important idea or issue out onto the Internet and it flowers thousands of times over. This is a key development in our evolution at this point in our history.

Central to this development is the degree to which people can communicate, form opinions, make judgments from available data, and then act upon them. The Internet is a medium that allows ideas to flow among thousands of channels. People are empowered not because one can get onto the Internet and get a product, read a newspaper or research out some knowledge. That thinking is from an old paradigm succinctly expressed in the saying: knowledge is power. The new paradigm is the ability to talk back (true interactivity), dialogue and go to whatever source an individual wants to choose. This is not to say there are thousands upon thousands of people out there engaged in political activism. There aren't.

There are legions of people who are out there ruminating and thinking, or engaging in conversation (or whatever activity one chooses). Many of these people are not restrained by the dictates of mass media which tell us what we must read, what is the story of the day, or what we must listen to on the radio or watch on TV. None of these media afford the independence of operation that the Internet allows. This is another reason why the Internet is developing into such a strong, world political force, not captured by boundaries, time, space or distance.

It is true that many in the world still very much reflect their religious beliefs, cultures, ethnic or political bias. Beyond this lies the opportunity to break away from the intellectual and emotional chains of the past and be free as an individual. And this is occurring on the Internet. However, even with these changes, there are still opportunities for governments themselves to benefit from the changes.

There are also efforts by many governments, worried about the potential freedoms a medium such as the Internet brings, to curtail both access and content on the Internet.

Because the Internet as a medium is becoming the tool through which the nature of democracy itself is changing and taking new shapes and forms, it is important that governments understand this phenomenon. Increasingly, public officials and elected politicians are going to be faced with not only an informed citizenry but a citizenry that wants to be engaged in the decision making process in some form or another. An analysis of the numerous groups springing up on the Internet on a multitude of issues illustrates that there are voices out there that governments are going to have to tap into.

The Internet has brought about a decentralization of power. In the wired world, individuals can now make their own choices as to which authorities and information sources they will accept.

This is leading to a greater democratization of knowledge, empowerment of the individual, and the potential for more informed interactions between the citizenry and organizations, including government. Moreover, since individuals now have ready access to a variety of information resources, organizations have to adopt new proactive measures to compile and disseminate information in a competitive information environment.

A citizenry that is able to seek and obtain information and knowledge from any place in the world through the Internet will, in all likelihood, also expect more from government. One of the means that people can collectively work together to bring about change is through the strategic gathering, absorbing and using of information.

Online groups and online activists, researchers and others involved as information professionals, instinctively understand this. It is the understanding of the nature of information and how it influences us as individuals that is going to bring the next big shift in society.

As the Internet takes hold in our daily lives, and begins to take a new and ubiquitous shape and form, the need for governments to develop information policies to suit the changing nature of these technologies is becoming more evident. In much of the developed world, the Internet is a communications force that is growing.

According to NUA plc, a company in Ireland, that tracks the growth of the Internet and the implication of our growing information technology infrastructure, as of the end of the year 2000, 60% of the population in the United States and Canada will have some form of online access to the Internet. This can be in the office, the home, an educational institute or some public space, such as libraries, community halls, Internet cafes and other public venues.

In the United Kingdom, over 50% of the population now enjoy some kind of Internet access. There, much of the growth of the Internet has been stimulated because many companies offer Internet access free. The citizen pays only for local calls.

In Europe, the whole question of measured rates is a serious issue, as many contend, this does impede not only access to the Internet, but, even if there is access, then the individual has to be careful about how long one is online. This is because the cost factor can act as an inhibitor to accessing the Internet and the amount of time spent online. However, despite these problems, there are now over 200 million people online around the world.

We are now awash with information in our new cyber environments. There are currently billions of pages out on the world wide web. There is so much information that no single search engine can go out and suck up all the information an individual might be seeking.

In fact, there is such a proliferation of information that many search engine companies now do not give total access to everything that is on the web. What some of the search engine companies are now doing is giving priority to companies who pay to have their company or organization show first on a search, when a given topic or key word is entered into their search engine. This is now giving an edge to those who can afford to pay the necessary fee to be at the top of the list. The world wide web is now so big that some web sites are not even getting joined to the network of networks because there might be a connection problem in their local area. Also, government and private organizations are now building web sites that can only be accessed through their own Intranets, or by having a specific address for a web site with a password to enter.

The world is at the fingertips of the citizen, but the new challenge is actually finding what is out there. The freewheeling, widely democratic, open, ubiquitous, and accessible Internet is still there, but the shadows of secrecy are beginning to move in. The danger exists that corporate dominance, with the economic rules of the market force at play, could inherently impede the free nature of the Internet over time.

When entering cyberspace, the challenges for the citizen who wants an open and accountable society, both from government and the private sector world, are now many. The success of our new information technology environments is going to depend on how much say and control citizens will have on information in the decade to come.

Information is shaping our world. We now live in the Digital Age, in which information, in a global knowledge economy, has become the supreme commodity. Information is not only a piece of barter for the business world to use for competitive and commercial value. Information is now a precious commodity for the citizen.

In our new Internet environments, citizens are increasingly demanding more privacy rights to protect their personal information. However, there is also a contradiction here, as at the moment, citizens are sharing and using personal and aggregate information more than ever before. But in a cyberspace environment, the citizen is becoming increasingly sophisticated in understanding the impact that information can have on one's life. The individual wants to ensure that one's own personal information is not abused.

The individual wants the ability to control his/her personal information environment in cyberspace. At the same time, the individual wants unfettered access to all manner of information.

But the sheer amount of information available, the ability to communicate information, and the value that individuals put on information, is bringing a new understanding of the nature of information itself. This understanding is also what is driving the new forces for change in the growing democracy online movement around the world.

Thus, on the side of freedom of information, the public is starting to demand more information for all facets of their lives. We see more data on labels of commercial products; shareholders demand more information about the activities of the companies in which they are investing (not just the usual "hyped" good news about the company's activities in the past year). Citizens are demanding and seeking more information about many activities in society.

The Information Age appears to be bringing more demands for accountability. In the years to come, the public will come to expect more and more accountability, in the form of enlightening information, from private sector organizations. The Internet is an open network, which has created open environments.

With this openness has come a demand for certain rights, to ensure the inherent democratic nature of the Internet is maintained. This idea is now spreading into society as a whole, resulting in demands for more and more accountability from all our public and private sector organizations.

Thus, it appears that the next wave of information rights will spread out to the private sector. As the average citizen becomes armed with more knowledge (or at least has the capacity to be armed with knowledge), then it will be private sector organizations, along with governments, who are going to have to become more forthcoming about the information held in their organizations.

The private sector here means not just large corporations or businesses, but rather all organizations, including non-profits. Just as privacy moved into the domain of the private sector thirty years ago, when Sweden passed the first data protection law in the world, so will freedom of information become a part of the private sector domain. The shape and form it takes will be different, but the providing of more information to society will occur.

We currently live in an age of individuals' rights, because in our current climate of the citizen as consumer, the individual is paramount. This will change, as the recognition dawns that it is also aggregate rights that strengthen the citizenry as a whole. As this idea flourishes, then privacy will now hold the same sway, and demands for information on a more sophisticated level will grow. Privacy will become a part of civil society's infrastructure. As the knowledge economy grows, and the knowledge professional comes to be seen as a powerful force in our society, so will the demands for wider swathes of information grow. It might seem at the moment that we already live in a world with too much information. This change of demand for information will be for "organized" information that informs, not overwhelms, the citizen.

Information is now an issue in a new form. Governments are also going to be subject to pressures from emerging information forces in society. For example, the secrecy of governments, at the moment, is defined to the degree that information is shared with the public.

The lack of efficacy of a freedom of information law is shown by the narrowness with which government exempts information from the public. Canada's information law is currently under review, because of the criticisms that the statute too much favours the public sector, and too much information is withheld on specious grounds.

Another reason for a review of the Canadian Access to Information Act is that it was developed in the late seventies, and passed by Parliament in 1982, before the emergence of new information technologies. But the challenge of governments now is not just to pass or amend freedom of information laws.In our new environments, we have to look at information as the force it has become in society.

Changing environments bring different attitudes. For example, as governments go online with electronic service delivery, more content is going to become available to the public. But it is not going to be enough to put information up on a web site. Any information is going to have to be organized.

In many cases, there is too much information on a web site, which makes the site virtually unusable by the citizen. Thus, information management is rising as a discipline within government. This is vital, so that policies can be evolved which ensure citizens are getting the information they need and want (not what someone 'thinks' the public want), while at the same time protecting individual privacy.

Once governments put content online, a policy issue will immediately emerge. The private sector learned this in the early days of the web. The growth of online marketing and ecommerce brought with it major privacy and copyright issues. For the citizen, who is going online for government information, if a request is rejected, the issue will become: why can't I have access?

In an information-intensive society, citizens want more from both governments and the private sector alike. The above is simply an overview of the emerging issues and problems. Solutions need to be sought, as these new technologies become even more persuasive forces in our society.

There are numerous ways that governments at the local, regional and national level can facilitate these new forms of democracy that are emerging. One is to take the example of Canada. The Canadian government, through their Community Access Program (CAP) has a goal to establish over 10,000 public access sites in rural and urban communities across Canada.

Launched in 1994, CAP has already established over 4,200 sites in approximately 3,000 rural and remote communities and is a key component of the government's "Connecting Canadians" strategy - aimed at making Canada the world's most connected nation." The program is now being expanded to include urban centres with populations over 50,000.

CAP matching funds of up to $17,000 per site are available to eligible applicants such as educational institutions, public libraries, community organizations, and municipal and territorial governments. The community funds can include cash or "in kind" contributions such as facilities, equipment and staffing of public access sites.

This is a good model to be followed not only by national governments but international organizations. If we are to handle the digital divide between those who have the opportunities to be online and the vast numbers of people who cannot necessarily afford the costs of going online, it is going to be essential to level the playing field.

In any populist democracy it is important that initiatives embrace all the people. At the moment it is estimated there are only between 150 and 200 million people online. These are small numbers where our world population has exceeded 6 billion people.

International organizations could also provide programs to educate people on usage of the Internet. Education then leads to individual usage. It will, naturally, vary from individual but through knowledge of how to use the Internet people can be participants in this new trend in democracy as they see fit. Such programs can embrace many peoples around the world and ensure that the users who most benefit are not just those in the affluent, industrialized countries. National Government should seek ways to engage their citizenry in the process of government. They can do this in many ways such as:

- making more information available online from government itself to ensure there is an informed citizenry;
- providing web sites that seek input from people on all manner of government programs and issues;
- developing listservs and discussion groups on important national issues and other means to engage the citizenry;
- providing grants to organizations seeking online democratic activities;
- developing local community projects that embrace all levels of society from the academic world, to businesses, large and small, to non-profit and volunteer organizations; this can encompass governments in developing countries;
- develop web sites that allow citizens easy access to web sites;
- ensure information on web sites is easily attainable, in a form understood by the citizen and can easily be downloaded;
- provide search engines and hot links to ensure the citizen gets what he or she wants in the right format from the right agency;
- in developing countries where access to the Internet is limited work to develop information policies that encompass all the citizens in the countries;
- develop programs to teach local leaders in the communities to become information facilitators;
- UNESCO to form a working group to develop a set of best Information Practices, that can be applied and used in developing countries.

The Internet is a medium that has allowed people to involve themselves in the democratic process in new and unique ways. Governments at all levels and international organizations will increasingly be impacted by these changes. Thus, there is also a need for awareness building within governments and international organizations of the changes that are occurring. This can be accomplished through educational and training programs.

3

Information as a Global Assets

The Information Revolution, and the Information Age that it engenders, is being defined by an on-going process of economic, social and political globalisation. While the term globalisation has become quite widespread, even in the popular media, there are confused and often conflicting definitions and conceptions of the phenomenon. In order for this concept to maintain any analytical usefulness, it must be unpacked, carefully defined and examined for its impact on society, the economy, and the world system.

At its most organic and fundamental level, globalisation is about the monumental structural changes occurring in the processes of production and distribution in the global economy. These structural changes are responses by many global enterprises that confront tremendous pressures and fantastic opportunities presented by the increased application and integration of advanced information and communications technologies (ICTs) into their core business processes. Through the application of information and communications technologies, enterprises have the ability to diminish the impact of space, time and distance. Global companies can break apart business functions that were previously thought to be best collocated (i.e. within the same geographic area), and spread them across the globe in a globally disarticulated labor and production process.

This aspect of globalisation requires the existence and development of an advanced information and communications infrastructure, based on a network of networks of telecommunications, broadcasting, computers, and content providers. This network of networks?a Global Information Infrastructure?currently does not exist. Such a GII should be a robust, global, broadband, high-capacity network, most likely based on fibre optic cable networks. The Internet and World Wide Web currently come closest to meeting these requirements. However, as sociologists Manuel Castells argues, "the Integrated Broadband Networks (IBN) envisioned in the 1990s could surpass substantially the revolutionary 1970s proposals for an Integrated Services Digital Network (ISDS)".

At a more conjunctural and secondary level, globalisation is affecting all of the social, political and economic structures and processes that emerge from this global restructuring. One critical issue that emerges from all of these restructuring processes is the central role of knowledge, education and learning for the success of the Global Information Society (GIS) and global information economy. Knowledge is becoming an increasingly important factor of production. More important, some analysts would argue, than land, labor and capital.

This chapter explores the contours of the on-going process of globalisation, including its alternative and contending perspectives. It also comments on its impact on society, the state, and the economy. Throughout this chapter, there is an underlying focus on the impact of globalisation on knowledge, education and learning and the promises and challenges of the Global Information Infrastructure--Global Information Society (GII-GIS) to meet the increasing needs and demands of the world?s citizens.

The global political economy is experiencing massive changes and fundamental internal and external restructuring. It has gone from a dynamic system which produced, for some, a "golden age" of capitalism in the 1950s to a system that is facing a global crisis. The current crisis is being foisted upon the world by a fundamental change in the underlying structures of production and distribution within the global economy.

Alain Lipietz argues that as a result of this restructuring a new development model is emerging. Since the 1950s, the dominant model for techno-economic development has been the Fordist?Taylorist development model. Fordism?Taylorism rested upon three major pillars. The first pillar was the factory system and mass production. The second pillar was the application of scientific management. And finally, the third pillar was the moving assembly line.

These practices enabled the Fordist?Taylorist development model to "more efficiently harness physical labor from huge masses of relatively unskilled shop-floor workers." This Fordist?Taylorist model was only fully implemented in the advanced industrialised countries which has tremendous implications for the developing countries within this current period of global economic restructuring.

The global system of production and distribution is now progressing from this Fordist?Taylorist development model to one based upon what Richard Kenney and Martin Florida call Innovation-Mediated Production. Innovation-Mediated Production, challenges significantly the Fordist?Taylorist development model and is based upon the blurring of the distinctions between mental and physical labor and the increase in the application of knowledge to the production process itself. This change is so significant that it represents a fundamental shift, for much of the world, in the underlying technological and economic paradigm (techno-economic paradigm) of industrial organization.

On the one hand, the highly industrialised countries of the world, as represented by the Organisation for Economic Cooperation and Development (OECD), are adapting to this techno-economic paradigm shift through various strategies, and high-levels of public and private sector cooperation. On the other hand, the developing countries are facing a tremendous tidal wave of changes, opportunities and challenges in this new era of globalisation and economic restructuring, which in many cases is overwhelming capacity.

The knowledge intensive nature of this development model?Innovation-Mediated production?requires firms to invest heavily in research and development (R&D), not as a luxury or solely to gain competitive advantage, but to survive. In some countries, this research system has been developed into a National System of Innovation, which harnesses the resources of the public sector, private sector, academic sector and non-governmental organizations. One area that has garnered a huge share of R&D expenditure in the developed countries has been optoelectronics.

Optoelectronics represents the fusion of photonics technologies (using photons as the delivery mechanism) with microelectronics (using electrons as the delivery mechanisms) "to attain greater efficiency in data processing and transmission than electronics can achieve by itself." The application of optoelectronics has produced radical new developments in information and communications technologies. This increased focus on optoelectronics is "drastically revolutionizing the communication system and [is] widely expected to form the next generation of information-based technologies." These new technologies have given us the Internet, World Wide Web, Integrated Systems Digital Networks (ISDN), Asynchronous Transfer Mode (ATM), Electronic Data Interchange (EDI), and a host of other technologies that have fueled the Information Revolution. In addition, the increased application of digitization techniques blurs the distinctions between telecommunications, computers, broadcasting and other high-technology sectors. Analysts have developed a concept to describe the blurring of lines between "once separate industries into an integrated digital marketplace."

The Optoelectronics Revolution, amongst many other components, facilitates what Jeffrey Henderson calls the "Global Option." By applying these new information and communications technologies, firms are now able to promote a globally disarticulated production and distribution process. This means that the various components of the production and distribution process?R&D, manufacturing, testing, information management, advertising, and marketing?need not be ir. the same geographic location. In fact, these various components can be, and are often, spread out on continents around the world. For example, R&D can take place on one continent, manufacturing on several different ones, testing on another continent, and information management on still another. The advertising and marketing of these products can take place on a global scale with niche marketing tactics?even if the public relations firm is located in a small remote country. All of these activities are currently taking place, they are increasing, and they are proceeding at the speed of light. Henderson calls this the "World Factory" phenomenon.

Global corporations, especially those competing in the converging high-technology industries, have increasingly expressed the tendency to utilize the new Innovation-Mediated development model and to explore the Global Option. The incessant technological development of the new techno-economic paradigm, the convergence of telecommunications, computers, and broadcasting, along with the increased pressures for global deregulation, liberalization and market-access have radically altered the global political economy and have undermined the existing the international telecommunications regime.

International regime theory, as developed in the social sciences, attempts to address the so-called "anarchy problematique." This intellectual construction addresses the ways in which "sovereign and equal" nation-states, operating in an anarchic world system in which there is no juridical or de jure authority over them attempt to address issues which are by their very nature transnational. Regime theory suggests that there are various mechanisms within the world system that facilitate the development of specific norms, principles, and values relating to the issue area and the mechanisms to enforce those norms, principles and values. Telecommunications is one of the issue areas around which one of the oldest and most successful international regimes has emerged. The International Telecommunication Union (ITU), has served as the centerpiece of this regime, with tremendous benefits flowing to national PTTs. Several social, economic, political and technological factors are converging to undermine this regime.

Globalisation and the Information Revolution present increasing difficulties for national states as they attempt to make choices about how to respond and allocate their scarce resources to confront this challenge. This challenge is particularly acute for African countries that are being bombarded with multiple "options" as to what actions and strategies are appropriate for their particular countries. As we have discussed above, knowledge as a factor of production within this new information-intensive economy, is gaining in importance in the era of globalisation. The education and learning paradigm around the world is under increasing pressure to better meet the demands of this new knowledge and information-intensive global economy.

These fundamental components of globalization set the context for this chapter. As these developments lurch forward, it is extremely important that social scientists, national-governments, non-governmental, international and regional organisations, and the private sector, attempt to understand the impact of globalisation on the global political economy and on local realities. The existing literature on globalization and the Information Revolution is to a large degree theoretical and overly speculative. There is a need for a clear theorization of globalization and the transformation occurring in the global economy which is grounded in an empirical analysis of local realities, including the knowledge, education and learning requirements for the information age.

Given the increasing economic globalisation and restructuring in the world political and economic systems,. and the requirements for knowledge and information within that system, educational needs (in terms of structure, function, curriculum and approach) at all levels, especially at the tertiary level, have changed. These educational requirements for the workforce of the future are extremely important. However, the systems developed for informal learning, specifically for adult learners to engage in life-long learning, are important as well.

There are significant contrasts between knowledge, education and learning. "Education is generally seen as a formal process of instruction, based on a theory of teaching, to impart formal knowledge (to one or more students)." However, the process of learning can occur, with or without formal institutional education. "Knowledge accumulation and the accumulation of skills for using ICTs will occur increasingly outside the traditional institutions of formal education. Learning in the workplace, and through collaborations that sometimes span the global and at other times involve tightly nit local communities with similar interests, will become more commonplace."

However, knowledge should not be limited to a select few. As the store of knowledge expands throughout the world, all of the world?s people should have as much access as possible. However, the "formal institutions of education that exist today, and even many of these in the planning stages in developing countries, are becoming less relevant to the requirements of emergent ?knowledge societies?." Mansell and Wehn argue that these countries must actively reshape their educational systems in ways that are "consistent with their national priorities." However, these national priorities must now take into consideration the fundamental changes occurring in the underlying structures of the global economy and new strategies for achieving competitive national advantage.

The role of knowledge within the economy is leading to a whole range of new industries and new developments in biotechnology, new materials science, informatics, computer science, etc. Within this new framework for knowledge, education and learning, there are at least ten components that should be included and or enhanced.

Some of the challenges for knowledge, education and learning in this period will be ability for today's learners to be more familiar and comfortable with abstract concepts and uncertain situations. Much of the academic environment today, presents students with ready-made problems and then asks them to solve them. The reality of the rapid-fire global economy, based on information and knowledge is that problems are rarely that clearly defined. It requires those seeking valuable employment to seek out problems, gather the necessary information, and make decisions and choices based on complex uncertain realities.

Much of the education and learning environment today is divided into very rigid academic disciplines, focused on discrete units of research. However, the emerging Information Society and global economy requires a holistic understanding of systems thinking, including the world system and business eco-systems.

Thus inter-disciplinary research approaches are seen as critical to achieving a more comprehensive understanding the complex reality currently facing the world system.

Symbols are highly abstracted manifestations of some concrete form of reality. Highly productive employment in today?s economy will require the learner to constantly manipulate symbols, such as political, legal and business terms and concepts (such as intellectual property rights), and digital money (in financial systems and accounting concepts). These "symbolic analysts," as Robert Reich calls them, are in high demand.

In the past, academic practitioners often saw themselves as wise "sages on the stage" delivering data, information, knowledge and wisdom to the eagerly awaiting students, whose minds were empty vessels waiting to be filled. However, if that reality were ever true, the world?s store of knowledge is increasing at such a monumental rate, that no single person can hope to adequately convey as comprehensive an understanding of a subject as is possible, or as could be absorbed by most students. The Global Information Infrastructure Commission (GIIC), an international, independent, non-governmental private sector organisation argues that:

The globalization of the economy and its concomitant demands on the workforce requires a different education that enhances the ability of learners to access, assess, adopt, and apply knowledge, to think independently to exercise appropriate judgment and to collaborate with others to make sense of new situations. The objective of education is no longer simply to convey a body of knowledge, but to teach how to learn, problem-solve and synthesize the old with the new.

There are a range of new technologies and new techniques engendered by the Information Revolution that allow for the production of new knowledge and the dissemination of data, information and knowledge. Some of these technologies include the Internet, World Wide Web, CD-ROM, and printed, audio, video and other electronic media forms. These new technologies allow for academic practitioners to move from being "sages on the stage" into the role of the "guide on the side" and assist students in gaining the skills and abilities required to acquire and utilise knowledge contained in various forms around the world.

The emerging economy is based on knowledge as a key factor of production, perhaps a factor more important than any other traditional factors of production. The kinds of industries emerging in the age of globalisation?such as biotechnology, new materials science, human genetics, advanced computing, artificial intelligence, and human/computer interfaces?demand that employees remain highly trained in science and technology. Research and development is a critical component, and many countries are trying to develop National Systems of Innovation (NSIs) that attempt to harness the combined resources of its academic institutions with the research enterprises within the public and private sectors. In these countries, universities will have to quickly adapt to the needs and provide a key component of such national systems.

The Fordist-Taylorist development model made strict separations between mental and physical labour. However, the new innovation-mediated paradigm requires a much more holistic approach to the business enterprise and valorizes the intellectual contributions of all employees. In fact, most observers would find it very difficult to make concrete distinctions between many Information Age-oriented manufacturing facilities and computer laboratories.

Closely related to the last point, is the need for employees in globalised enterprises to be able to work closely in teams. Working in teams requires students to develop skills in group dynamics, compromise, debate, persuasion, organisation, leadership and management skills. Most academic institutions and programmes are set up to do the opposite, to force students to think only of themselves and their own personal development, perhaps with some very limited group work.

Again, closely related to the last point, is the need for enhanced virtual and networked activity. Not only should students learn to work in teams; but also they should learn to work in global networked virtual teams. These global virtual teams are being used increasingly in industry and international organisations for R&D activities. Chris Dede argues that "Computer-supported collaborative learning (CSCL) enhances team performance through tools for communicating each person?s ideas, structuring group dialogue and decision making, recording the rationales for choices, and facilitating collective activities."

As command and control systems disintegrate around the world, academic institutions must become less rigid and more flexible in their attempt to meet the varied needs of learners and the global economy. This includes variety in time, place, approach and curriculum offerings. As new issues and industries emerge within the global economy, academic course offerings should be adapted to reflect these new knowledge, education and learning requirements.

Using advanced information and communications technologies, a new system of knowledge, education and learning should apply a wide range of synchronous and asynchronous activities that aid the professor and student in breaking the boundaries of space and time. Synchronous activities can include real-time lectures (featuring audio, presentations, web sites, and even video), quizzes and group discussions; all of which can occur with the instructor being at the same location or even a different location from the learner. Asynchronous activities can include archived lectures (in audio and video), and other archived course material that can be accessed at nearly anytime, anyplace.

To meet the knowledge, education and learning challenges and opportunities of the Information Age, the GIIC argues:

It is not, however, sufficient anymore to raise the efficiency of the existing systems of education and improve the quality of their components. Even the best of them have served another set of demands for another age. Graduates of these systems, to varying degrees, now find themselves deficient in knowledge as well as cognitive skills that are necessary for the increasingly sophisticated living environment and for the ever-evolving labor market. More importantly, knowledge based businesses often complain that graduates lack the capacity to learn new skills and assimilate new knowledge.

To meet these challenges and to reap the benefits of the opportunities presented by globalisation, active responses should occur within the public and private sectors at national, regional and international levels.

At a national level, these requirements for knowledge, education and learning should be addressed with policy approaches that: (1) allow as many people as possible to engage in productive healthy forms of employment that enhances their quality of life; and (2) meet the increasing demands of global enterprises operating within the global economy.

Developing countries are behind significantly in the information infrastructure required to generate and disseminate knowledge. One concept that could address these concerns is the emerging vehicle of Multimedia, Multipurpose Community Information Centres (MPCICs or Telecentres). Current research indicates that these centres could serve as effective vehicles for enhancing the knowledge, education and learning opportunities for communities in emerging economies.

Within the private sector, at national levels, there are efforts to strengthen the partnership between the private sector and public sector in the delivery of education and learning. Again, the GIIC argues that there are specific roles for the private sector within this framework, because the educational establishment may not be able to redefine itself sufficiently to meet the requirements of the new information-intensive economy. The Commission sees three critical roles for the private sector in the education sector.

The first recommended role for the private sector is the rethinking of education. The Commission argues that. "Since its success depends to a large extent on the product of the educational system, the private sector should engage in the rethinking of education to meet the demands of the age of globalization and information by providing, systematically, input into the analytical and decision making processes in areas such as strategic shifts, curricula, restructuring, standards, and evaluation."

Collaboration in training for the new economy is a second role recommended by the GIIC for the private sector in education. This recommendation springs from an assumption that the training within private institutions has the following advantages: (1) employers can train workers quickly and place them into positions; (2) training costs are lower; (3) the technology in these enterprises is usually advanced; (4) quick responses to the needs of the marketplace.

Finally, the GIIC suggests that the provision of educational services is a critical role for the private sector in education. It argues that the public sector will be unable to continue bearing the major financial responsibility for the financing and provision of education.

With the escalating demands and the diversification of avenues of dissemination of knowledge, governments will not be able to be the sole providers of education. There will be more opportunities for the private sector to provide educational services with a competitive edge based on efficiency, flexibility, management style, and information technology. The obvious domain is at the secondary and tertiary levels as well as in the fields of skill development and upgrading and lifelong learning.

The GIIC believes that it is in a unique position, "at the intersection between technology and private businesses," to make a positive contribution to promoting these concepts around the world. It suggests the following responses for the GIIC in collaboration with its members and international partners.

1. Create and support a forum to connect scientists, information technologists, policy makers, and practitioners for the purpose of rethinking education in the age of globalization and information.
2. Support mechanisms for the exchange of ideas and experiences in the use of educational technologies.
3. Encourage explorations, experimentation to push the frontiers of the potential of information technologies and communications for more effective learning.
4. Engage in the design of pilot "learning communities" that expands the time and space dimensions of education.
5. Encourage, and engage in, collaborative schemes for the development of educational curriculum-related software that can be used worldwide to achieve economies of scale and expertise.
6. Support the design of information infrastructure that is most appropriate for education and that is cost-effective, implementable and sustainable at large scales.

Whether or not the GIIC engages in these activities, it is clear that at global, regional and national levels, within both the public and private sectors, there is a need for concrete responses in knowledge, education and learning to the challenges and opportunities presented by the age of globalisation. The next section focuses on key examples at each of these levels.

Globalization is a very real phenomenon that is transforming the world economic system including nearly all aspects of production, distribution and other business processes. With the emergence of a new development model, particularly in the highly industrialised economies, knowledge and information take on increasing importance. Thus, the era of globalisation has tremendous concomitant implications for knowledge, education and learning.

This chapter has argued that one implication of this transformation is that a new system of knowledge, education and learning will include many components that do not exist in the current educational model. The new system of knowledge, education and learning should include the following ten key components.

1. A focus on abstract concepts;
2. Uses a holistic, as opposed to linear, approach;
3. Enhances the student?s ability to manipulate symbols;
4. Enhances the student?s ability to acquire and utilise knowledge;
5. Produces an increased quantity of scientifically and technically trained persons;
6. Blurs the distinction between mental and physical labour;
7. Encourages students to work in teams;
8. Uses virtual teams around the world;
9. Is an agile and flexible system; and
10. Break the boundaries of space and time.

In addressing the challenges posed by globalisation, tremendous levels of cooperation are needed, between the public and private sectors, and between global, regional and national organisations. The Global

Information Infrastructure Commission is making some headway at forging such a framework for global cooperation.

Information as a "global public good"

"New information and communication technologies are driving globalisation—but polarising the world into the connected and the isolated." The appropriate use of information and communications technology has the potential to deliver massive benefits in terms of human development and to be a fast-track to knowledge-based growth. The reality for the bulk of the world's population is that these benefits remain well beyond their grasp, with most information and communication technologies ("ICT") being concentrated in only a few countries; for example, only 55 countries account for 99% of global spending on information technology. The result is that, "the global gap between haves and have-nots—between know and know-nots, is widening". This phenomenon is what is known as the "digital divide".

In response to the concerns raised by the digital divide, UNESCO (among its other initiatives) passed a resolution at its November 1999 General Conference urging all Member States to, "promote free and universal access to public domain information for the purposes of education, science and culture."

The intention of this chapter is to stimulate debate and suggestions on how UNESCO, Member States and other appropriate agencies could recommend or implement strategies and actions to give effect to this Resolution. The challenge is to determine how governments and civil society can discharge their responsibility to make information which is considered to be a "global public good" universally available for educational, cultural and social needs.

In the context of the global information society, the phrases "public domain", "public content" and "global public good", are often used interchangeably (depending on the syntax). Of these phrases, the most pervasive term is "public domain information". This is quite a nebulous concept. It is very hard to define because historically it has had different meanings depending on the context in which it is used. The meaning has also evolved over time.

The phrase "public domain" has its origins in physical space that, historically, equated to publicly owned land. In some jurisprudence it was defined as land owned by the Government.

The case law, what little there is of it on this topic, is not constrained to notions of Government or Crown ownership, but with the broader concept of publicly owned property.

These two threads, of State ownership (whether Government or Crown) and publicly owned property, converge and are then extrapolated in another Canadian court decision in the following definition, "The public domain is therefore defined as the collection of immovable and movable properties belonging to the State and the properties appropriated to public purposes belonging to municipalities and other legal persons established in the public interest. Whatever is not included therein constitutes the private domain". This definition of "public domain" broadens its meaning beyond land and tangible property, as well as introduces another theme, that is the concept of "public purposes" and "public interest". The concept of public domain therefore takes on a gloss which in current usage (in the appropriate context) has evolved into the concept of information as a "global public good".

In modern usage, the analogy is often drawn between public domain information in the global information society and the concept of "commons" or "commonage". This analogy is another means of introducing the notion of sharing, equal access and collective or communal rights. Both phrases, "public domain" and "commons", have similar origins and historical definition.

A "commons" was a tract of land owned or used jointly by the residents of the community, usually a central square or park in a city or town. Under the law, "commons" was the right or liberty, in common with other persons, to take profit from the land or waters of another, as by pasturing animals on another's land (common of pasturage) or fishing in another's waters (common of piscary) . Even without this shared origin, the term "public domain" conveys the notion of "public purpose" and "public interest", for example, the right of the public to passage or use of a highway , and therefore the sense of some kind of collective or communal rights or interest in the "domain". This is very appropriate given that, in the context of the global information society, it is implicit that the citizens of the world have a legitimate interest in accessing "public domain information", also known as the "information commons".

There is also an interesting and relevant analogy in common law where, if a person uses the highway (which is a public domain) not for the purpose of passage but to interfere with the lawful use of the land by its owner, that person will have committed a tort (civil wrong). This court decision states that, "subject to these rights of the public, the owner is entitled to all his rights as owner and can sue anyone who interferes with those rights" . In other words, the fact that the public has an interest in the "public domain" (in the form of the right of passage on the highway) does not exclude other proprietary rights, such as those of the "owner" of the land.

There are modern day analogies with this reasoning in that it is possible for information to be "in the public domain", in the sense that it has been made publicly available and is not subject to confidentiality, while still remaining subject to proprietary rights in the form of the copyright of the author or publisher. It is interesting to note that the word "domain" still has connotations of a place or a space. Historically, a domain was a public space or land, just like a commons. In the context of the World Wide Web, a domain is a virtual space.

The confusion over the meaning of "public domain" probably arises because there are in fact two historical meanings of the term. The first is as discussed above, namely, public land. The second meaning refers to the status of a literary work or an invention whose copyright or patent has expired or that never had such protection. Therefore, when the term "public domain information" is used in the context of intellectual property rights, it can probably be assumed that it is referring to public domain works as meaning those that may be used without infringing copyright. This approach has been extended to cover public domain software or technology, as being that which is available without limitation on its subsequent distribution. Therefore, public domain software has been defined as software which is not protected by copyright; it is often distributed via mail order or copied from public bulletin boards.

The most common usage of "public domain" in respect of information, is in the context of the common law on the action for breach of confidence. This is not to be confused with any rights derived from copyright. The legal protection for confidential information, under the common law of contract and in equity, does not extend to matters that are regarded as already being "in the public domain". This is interpreted as with other qualifiers of the term "confidential information" as meaning, not available to the public. Such information will be deemed not to be confidential regardless of whether or not it was copyrightable.

The concept of "in the public domain", as being a reason why information cannot be subject to an obligation of confidentiality (nor be a trade secret), has been applied within the Agreement on Trade Related Aspects of Intellectual Property Rights ("TRIPS").

In particular, Article 39 (TRIPS), rather than attempting to define what is "public domain", approaches the situation from the converse by setting out the categories of information which are not disclosed (confidential) and in that sense are not in the public domain. The focus is on the confidential elements of information which justify protection as proprietary information, but based on obligations of confidence and not by virtue of its patent or copyright status.

In terms of modern day usage, it is possible to isolate some common threads. The most common quality of public domain information is that it is not subject to confidentiality. There are two other themes which are often (but not always) present.

In some contexts, such as for public domain software, the concept is synonymous with no controls or constraints on its subsequent use (for example, not subject to intellectual property protection). The other theme is that the term often implies notions of public purpose or benefit or interest, that is, "public good".

The phrase "global public good" is often used in discussions on the creation of global knowledge. Any attempts at definition are often couched in economic terms. For example, the underlying presumption of information as a "global public good", is that there are limits on the marketability of knowledge. Its saleability is limited by two features which distinguish it from more traditional goods or commodities. The first is what is described by economists as "nonrivalrous"; namely, one person's use of a piece of knowledge does not preclude its use by another.

The quote which is often used to illustrate this concept is that of Thomas Jefferson, "He who receives an idea from me, receives instruction himself without lessening mine; as he who lights his taper at mine, receives light without darkening me". The second characteristic of knowledge is that it is "non-excludable", in the sense that once it is in the public domain it is very difficult for its creator to prevent others from using that knowledge.

These two properties of knowledge have been described as analogous to the main characteristics of a public good; the other similarity is that these features make it possible for people to use knowledge without paying for it. This is one aspect which distinguishes knowledge from information which is copyrightable; in respect of the latter, it is only possible to have copyright in the expression of an idea, whereas the facts and the ideas themselves cannot be protected by copyright. Even if they are published, the facts and ideas are "in the public domain" and may be reused under copyright law.

Certain types of knowledge are regarded as being of such global import, with the potential to impact significantly on human advancement, that they are often associated as information which is a "global public good". The most common illustration is basic research, particularly where no one country or private organisation had the incentives to undertake the necessary research to create the knowledge.

As there is no margin or cost to an additional person using the knowledge, and because the exclusion of other users is either impossible or regarded as undesirable (where the costs of the resulting under-utilisation of the knowledge would outweigh the benefit), efficiency dictates that the supply of such knowledge or information requires international collective action.

A very topical example is the mapping of the human genetic code, where two teams of competing scientists have been collaborating on the later stages of their research. The resulting knowledge is what many would regard as fulfilling the economic definition of information as a "global public good". The intellectual property status of this phenomenal discovery is as yet unresolved, especially given the strong opposition by the Human Genome Project team and others to the prospect of this knowledge being patented.

The history of the term "public domain" shows that it has never had a particularly clear or absolute meaning. There have evolved, however, common understandings of what is meant by "public domain information", when it is used in various contexts, such as where there are pre-existing rights in respect of an activity, a benefit, or for categories of information content. The current range of meanings and usage include the following:

— Information which is neither secret nor subject to an obligation of confidentiality (eg. it has been published or is a matter of widespread public knowledge, and in these ways has been made publicly available). Note that such public domain information may still be subject to copyright.

— Where there are no applicable intellectual property rights (eg. the protections afforded by copyright, patent or design registration have expired). Note that where information has not been copyrighted or patented, there may still be stakeholders with an interest or rights in that information (eg. see the following category).

— Anonymous works, provided there is no infringement of any other stakeholder's interest (eg. the anonymous information is not subject to indigenous heritage rights or does not deal with personal information which would otherwise be protected under data protection or privacy laws).

— Copyright information to which the "fair use" exemption applies.

— Factual material (eg. research data). Note that this assumes the facts do not amount to a format or collation and therefore are not subject to copyright, and have not been protected by patent or design registration. To be public domain information, the factual material must not be subject to some other control (eg. to an obligation of confidence, national security secrecy, or be grounds for non-disclosure under freedom of information ("FOI") laws).

— Ideas, (eg. the results of scholarship which have been made public to enable other scholars to leverage off this knowledge). Note that the publication of an idea, because it is an "expression" of the idea, may still be subject to copyright and therefore might not be in the public domain. This category cannot include those ideas which have been patented as an invention.

— Deposits and collections in public libraries, archives and museums. Note that this public domain information may still be subject to certain constraints, such as conditions on retrieval, fees or subscriptions, or copyright.

— Metadata, being data about data, (eg. the information generated within a library about its collections, indexing and retrieval systems).

— Official information or content held or produced by government and made available: under government policy; by the courts as a matter of public policy; under FOI laws. Note that the disclosure of such information may still be constrained if it is covered by an exception to an FOI law. The publication of this type of "public content" may also be subject to Crown copyright.

— Information where either its availability or disclosure is seen as "for the public good" in the sense that it is in the public interest (eg. where the creator or an appropriate authority has determined that any private interest in the information is outweighed by a greater public interest in its availability). The circumstances of this information may range from knowledge derived from scholarship and research, court decisions interpreting the public interest in disclosure, or information on wrong-doing such as under a statutory "whistleblowing" (protected disclosures) regime.

— The creation of certain types of knowledge which can be categorised as a "global public good" (eg. where no one country or private sector organisation has the incentive or resources to undertake the necessary research to create this particular type of knowledge, but the gap has been filled by an international institution). An illustration is the application of agriculture research, where permitting the creation of private intellectual property rights is either inappropriate given the nature of the knowledge or information or else the cost (being the under-utilisation of that knowledge if kept private) would outweigh the benefit. The efficient supply of such information may require international collective action.

— Information which historically has been treated as collective or communal information (eg. traditional medicinal remedies), provided such information is not subject to the control of any guardians or custodians. Note that indigenous heritage (folklore) should not be assumed to be in the public domain. Other examples include publicly funded initiatives with the clearly stated aim of delivering public benefits, although again there may be a guardian (eg.

such as a trustee) retaining a certain amount of control over the dissemination of the information. Although there may be a presumption in favour of the information being in the public domain, it is not necessarily the case.

— Information, the circumstances of which indicate an intention by its developers or custodians to make it publicly available. Examples include: publicly funded developments with an undertaking to publish results; published Standards; news and other journalistic publications or broadcasts; private sector (business and industry) communications to the public (eg. consumer codes, terms and conditions of doing business, policies). Note that to the extent that any of these categories contain an expression of an idea or a formatting or collation of data, the publication or other works may still be subject to copyright law.

There is no one definition of "public domain information". Depending on its context, this concept of an "information commons" may embody any one or all of the above categories. If information is in the public domain, it cannot be assumed to be to the exclusion of all other interests or controls. This is consistent with its historical interpretation. It would be prudent to qualify the intended meaning of the term if its use is restricted to a specific instance or subset of its potential uses. The common thread is that if information is put into the public domain to become part of the information commons, it is being made publicly available, although there may be conditions on its use (whether in the form of copyright restrictions, subscription payments, qualifying criteria under FOI laws, or pre-conditions and rules as to its retrieval).

In the context of the global information society and the objective of universal access, "public domain information" potentially embodies all of the above categories. The objective is to close the gap between the information rich and information poor, which means expanding the amount of and quality of the information in the public domain and then facilitating equitable access for all citizens to the knowledge and benefits to be derived from that information commons.

Importance of Public Domain Information

The Human Development Report 1999, of the United Nations Development Programme (UNDP), has many disturbing statistics on the digital divide. For example, the Report states that:

— As at mid 1998, industrial countries (with less than 15% of the global population) had 88% of Internet users; North America (with less than 5% of all people) had more than 50% of Internet users; South Asia had less than 1% of the Internet users.

— In terms of access to the network society, only 2% of the world's population has "stepped into the loop". A quarter of all countries have not yet achieved the minimum teledensity threshold of one telephone per 100 people. Most telephones in developing countries are in the capital city, despite the majority of people living in rural areas. Connections are poor and the costs prohibitive.

— Internet connection and running costs average one hundred dollars per month in several African countries, compared with ten dollars in the United States.

— Adult literacy in 1995 was less than 40% in 16 countries and primary school enrolments were less than 80% in 24 countries. By contrast, globally, 30% of Internet users have at least one university degree.

– The findings of national Internet surveys in 1998 and 1999 , illustrate that income buys access (the example given was that to buy a computer, it will cost the average Bangladeshi more than eight years income, compared with one month's wage for the average American). The Internet is dominated by men and youth. Ethnic minorities, non-English speakers, women, the elderly, rural dwellers, and the poor, are being excluded from participation in the global information revolution. They are being denied the economic opportunities available to those with the capacity to create knowledge and to access the network society; "poor people and poor countries risk being pushed to the margin in this proprietary regime controlling the world's knowledge"

If knowledge creation is the key to human advancement, it follows that increasing public domain information, and facilitating universal (and equitable) access to that information, is fundamental to human well-being and to remedying the imbalances between the developing and the industrialised countries, and between disadvantaged and information rich communities.

In attempting to close the gap in the digital divide, there are many challenges. These include balancing other competing but legitimate interests. The difficulty in defining what is meant by "public domain information" illustrates this balancing exercise. Most of the categories of public domain information discussed above have unclear boundaries and are in no way absolute. There are often many stakeholders in the same piece of information, each with a legitimate interest. The regime of intellectual property rights is an obvious example of a legitimate interest in information, discussed in paragraph 4. The grounds for claiming ownership in information are not necessarily exclusive of another's claim, nor do they guarantee priority (as between claims). It is possible for many parties or stakeholders to compete for rights to the same item of information. Possession does not necessarily confer a greater right or responsibility, for example, where the holder is merely the custodian of the information (as is inherent in the proposals for specialist Aboriginal copyright collecting societies) .

Given the daunting challenge of the digital divide, it is imperative that the focus on public domain information looks for strategies and actions to broaden and expand the proportion of global knowledge which can be categorised as public domain information. This information has to be made publicly available, especially to those disenfranchised by the "fault lines" of information rich, information poor. It is imperative that all peoples can participate in the global information society and maximise the potential for human advancement. These are the concepts implicit in universal access. The provision of public domain information must be efficient and fair. The following discussion considers some specific issues which arise in the context of public domain information and achieving universal access, with a view to stimulating ideas on specific measures to achieve the aims of the Information for All Programme.

There is a significant tension between the increasing use of intellectual property rights ("IPR") to entrench private ownership in information and the need to expand the information commons and to access this public domain information. Private rights, (IPR), have to be balanced against the other arguments in favour of making information publicly available and removing the restrictions on its reuse, as would be imposed if the information is subject to, for example, patent or copyright protection. The economics of intellectual property rights protection, and its significant role in the long term creation of knowledge, is described in a World Bank Discussion Paper on the topic as follows, "Intellectual creations have some characteristics of public goods.

The blueprint for a new machine, the computer code for a software application, the script for a play, or a television broadcast can be simultaneously consumed by many economic agents at zero (or at a very low) marginal cost. In short, the cost of reproduction of intellectual creation is typically a fraction of the cost of production. Although pricing at marginal cost would maximise consumer welfare from a static perspective, it would curtail incentives for investing in the creation of new intellectual works or improving existing knowledge. By granting temporary exclusive rights, IPRs are intended to allow property holders to price their products above marginal cost and to recoup the initial knowledge - or information - generating investments."

The Discussion Paper recognises the implicit tension between intellectual property rights and public domain or public good objectives. By granting exclusive rights, intellectual property regimes can restrict the diffusion of knowledge and information, using patents as an example. It notes that monopolistic or oligopolistic behaviour among intellectual property owners can lead to less than optimal dissemination of new knowledge and information. However, these negatives are seen as the legitimate trade-off or compromise related to intellectual property protection, where enhanced market power allows intellectual property owners to recover their initial information and knowledge-generating investments.

It is also possible to argue that intellectual property rights can contribute to the diffusion and creation of knowledge. An example is the patent claim where in exchange for temporary exclusive rights, inventors may have an incentive to disclose knowledge to the public that might otherwise remain secret. By enforcing IPR standards, it is possible for developing countries to gain access to foreign markets and technologies, through direct investment and knowledge transfer, including outsourcing, licensing or joint venture arrangements. However, there are serious concerns that the international IPR framework under TRIPS has shifted the bargaining power towards content producers and is increasing the knowledge gap by slowing the rate of adaptation.

Despite the validity of the economic incentives argument, which supports the use of IPR regimes, there is an emerging trend which has disturbing implications for knowledge diffusion and human development. The asset value of information is now well recognised. There is a clear link between control over information and economic returns. We live in an era of unprecedented technological development. In the past twenty years there has been a significant growth in the filing of patent claims. Intellectual property claims are concentrated in a very few industrialised countries. The international IPR regime, in the form of the TRIPS Agreement, has significantly tightened the controls over the use and enforcement of IPR. The predicament is well summarised by the Human Development Report, "Globalisation's rules have set off a race to lay claim to knowledge. A global map for the technologies is being drawn up faster than most people are able to understand the implications—let alone respond to them - and faster than anyone's certainty of the ethical and developmental impacts".

The Report identifies a number of other concerning trends. In defining research agendas, the priorities are determined by the return on investment, rather than public need. This has significant implications in the areas of biotechnology and pharmaceuticals. There is a fear that tighter intellectual property rights could raise the price of technology transfer and block developing countries from dynamic knowledge sectors, such as computer software and generic drugs. Patent laws do not cater for the protection of indigenous knowledge and heritage, exposing these communities to exploitation by others. The cultural diversity of these different ownership systems, and the way innovation is created and shared, is not recognised by current IPR. The result of these trends has been summarised as follows, "As trade, patents and copyright determine the paths of technology—and of nations—questioning today's arrangements is not just about economic flows. It is about preserving biodiversity. Addressing the ethics of patents on life. Ensuring access to health care. Respecting other culture's forms of ownership. Preventing a growing technological gap between the knowledge-driven global economy and the rest trapped in its shadows."

The "fair use" doctrine and public domain information. These emerging trends pose significant challenges for those who are trying to redress the resulting global imbalances. There are a number of other issues which are also significant to the preservation of an information commons. One of these issues is the erosion of the "fair use" doctrine. Any undermining of this doctrine is of concern because it is one of the sources of public domain information.

The fair use doctrine usually allows re-use of copyrighted work without copyright infringement, for the purposes of critique, commentary, scholarship or research. Many legal systems then apply various tests or factors as a guide to whether or not a proposed use will fall within these statutory categories of fair use. The scope of the fair use exception is unclear and so it has been left to the courts in many jurisdictions to define the boundaries of what amounts to fair use and is therefore non-infringing. Some court decisions have seriously undermined the scope of this exception.

The origin of the fair use exception is directly relevant to the concepts underlying public domain information. Copyright is intended to advance learning and knowledge by creating an incentive system to induce authors to create and disseminate their works. However, the fair use exception is a more direct intervention or redistribution of rights to ensure access and equity for socially beneficial purposes. Access for research, education and critique purposes, via fair use, is seen as a public benefit and is the price of the limited statutory privilege available through copyright protection. In terms of the need to preserve the "public domain", and to build a knowledge society through equitable access, it is essential to preserve the fair use exception in copyright law.

Unfortunately, the development of Automatic Rights Management technology ("ARM") to monitor the exchange of digital information and to implement a user pays system for accessing and reusing protected information, could have a radical impact on the effectiveness of the fair use doctrine as a means of creating public domain information.

Instead of seeking protection through cumbersome and expensive copyright actions, it is now possible for a content producer to use technologies (such as ARM) to receive payment and to rely on standardised one-to-one licensing contracts to impose restrictions on the subsequent use of that information.

In this way, the public law of fair use can be bypassed. The substitution of licensing controls in the place of a codified fair use exemption means there is no obligation to consider the grounds (of fair use) which justify copying. The concern is that where content producers can exit copyright law in favour of contract, then the public bargain articulated through the fair use doctrine is seriously undermined.

The control available through licensing could also allow a form of private censorship; the content producer has the ability through the contract to prohibit certain subsequent uses which would otherwise have been authorised under the fair use doctrine. The information which is made available through fair use can be considered to be public domain information. It is unknown how much of the information protected by licensing, rather than under copyright, will fall into the public domain. These developments could pre-empt the fair use doctrine and abrogate the balance which most copyright laws seek to achieve.

A notable response to the perceived appropriation of knowledge through private IPR, has been the emergence of the "copyleft" movement in the software industry; this mechanism uses a mix of private contract law (licensing) and statutory copyright protection in an effort to open up the knowledge base within the software development industry. Copyleft involves the information "owner" using its contract or licensing power to ensure that subsequent users of that same information cannot constrain its re-use or further development. An example of copyleft is the development and popularity of open source code, such as for computer operating systems. It is becoming an increasingly powerful tool to counter the exclusiveness of some content producers.

The time may be right for international co-operation on what shared conceptions of public benefit or welfare justify reconsidering the framework of entitlements and contract rules that support the existing information market. Content producers and organisations representing major copyright industries have a strong vested interest in approaches to intellectual property which strengthen notions of property, rather than recognising the need to balance competing rights or interests.

There are a number of initiatives that could be considered in addressing the tension between the overuse of IPR and the imperative of resisting any further erosion of public domain information. There are also certain strategies and actions which might actually increase the amount of information in the public domain. These might include:

— Analyse the appropriateness or otherwise of adapting the fair use doctrine to intellectual property licensing, to give effect to the public bargain that is articulated in public copyright law.

— Promote research on other economic models for valuing information. Rather than assessing value purely in terms of individual preferences and in neo-classical market models, there should be further consideration of the impact of knowledge creation on progress (in both economic and social terms) and whether the overall value of that knowledge can be realised for society.

— On a project basis, identify information which is a global public good and therefore should not be available for patenting (eg. the outputs from mapping the human gene). In respect of working within the parameters of the international IPR regime, an alternative might be to promote partnerships between the public and private sectors to ensure sufficient funding as appropriate incentives for knowledge creation. In return for public funding, certain outputs of this knowledge creation process could subsequently be placed in the public domain. Patent protection could be available up to a certain level of return on investment or in respect of some applications but not others, beyond which certain knowledge must then be placed in the public domain. The issue of incentives could be addressed by contingent loans or outright purchases of IPR rights.

— Promote research which uses empirical evidence to investigate the links between IPR protection and innovation (eg. to resolve the current debate over whether or not patents are still the best way to promote innovation in new technologies).

— Promote credible studies of alternative methods of innovation, such as the copyleft movement, with particular emphasis on its efficiencies and economics. Consider alternative approaches to innovation based on sharing, open access and communal innovation.

— Ensure that reviews of existing IPR legislation (eg. any WTO review of the TRIPS Agreement) include an assessment of the social and economic implications of the increasing use of patents.

— Encourage developing countries to participate actively in international negotiations on IPR issues. A case can be made that new technological developments, such as in biotechnology and ICT, has introduced new issues for negotiation and raises concerns that were either not understood or failed to be addressed at the time of the initial negotiation or signing of these international agreements.

— The digitisation of print collections and archives may require special initiatives to ensure that in respect of copyrighted works, this process does not amount to "publication" which could infringe intellectual property rights.

Indigenous Heritage Rights

A common misconception is that indigenous cultural property, or folklore, is public domain information. Historically, the assumption has been that because such knowledge or information was never subject to any intellectual property right claim, that information could be appropriated by others. A more respectful view is that public domain information should not be presumed to include the works of folklore or indigenous intellectual and cultural property ("heritage").

The difficulty is that many indigenous cultures approach the guardianship of their heritage from the perspective of collective or communal rights. In contrast, IPR are essentially private economic rights and are therefore a very foreign concept for many indigenous peoples. There is an emerging trend of indigenous peoples feeling the need to file design and patent claims to prevent exploitation by others and inappropriate uses of their cultural icons and images. In doing so, they are being forced to adopt a legal paradigm which runs completely counter to their own "ownership" structures of collective or communal rights. The other theme which emerges when considering indigenous heritage, is the concept of guardianship where the indigenous people are the custodians of wider collective property. The concept of collective or communal rights should not be confused with public rights of access.

The focus on indigenous rights has been prompted by concerns over the culturally offensive use of indigenous heritage, the need for biodiversity conservation, and for the sustainable use of resources. However, as indigenous peoples have grappled with the tension between IPR and their cultural and philosophical approach to their heritage, very few have been able to resist the economic opportunities presented by the branding of their own designs, images, icons and traditional and customary knowledge. Indigenous people desire the right to control the use of their imagery and other taonga (precious things), the right to be consulted over the use of their heritage and the creation of some means of identifying and thereby protecting their cultural property; they also demand the right to negotiate the economic benefit which others may derive from the use of their cultural and intellectual property.

In some indigenous cultures, certain customary knowledge is either secret or sacred. This would create an obvious barrier to such information being treated as in the public domain (quite apart from the above issues of self-determination).

Another aspect of the role of public domain information in respect of indigenous heritage is that, where there is a collective or communal ownership structure, the implication is that this knowledge will be made available to a very wide number of people and in that sense may be publicly available. However, for as long as the indigenous people are a subset of the wider population, this availability will not equate to unrestricted universal access.

The special position of indigenous rights has been addressed in a number of international conventions and protocols (for example, the Draft Declaration on the Rights of Indigenous Peoples 1993). These documents resist any interpretation that indigenous heritage or folklore can be equated with public domain information; for example, Article 24 of the Draft Declaration states that, "Indigenous peoples have the right to their traditional medicines and health practices, including the right to the protection of vital medicinal plants, animals and minerals". Article 29 states that, "Indigenous peoples are entitled to the recognition of the full ownership, control and protection of their cultural and intellectual property. They have the right to special measures to control, develop and protect their sciences, technologies and cultural manifestations".

There are numerous measures that are required to protect the special position of indigenous cultural and intellectual property. The significance of these measures for public domain information lies in the subtleties of the custodian arrangements articulated by indigenous peoples in respect of their heritage and their acknowledgement of the legacy of this customary knowledge for all humanity. This is illustrated by the Mataatua Declaration on Cultural and Intellectual Property Rights of Indigenous Peoples.

This Declaration seeks recognition that indigenous peoples are the exclusive owners of their culture and intellectual property. However, the preamble goes on to affirm, that, "the knowledge of the Indigenous Peoples of the World is of benefit to all humanity" recognises that indigenous peoples, "are willing to offer it [their traditional knowledge] to all humanity provided their fundamental rights to define and control this knowledge are protected by the international community; insist that the first beneficiaries of indigenous knowledge (culture and intellectual property rights) must be the direct indigenous descendants of such knowledge". Under its recommendations, the Declaration asks for recognition that, "indigenous peoples are the guardians of their customary knowledge and have the right to protect and control dissemination of that knowledge".

The implication of indigenous statements such as the above is that indigenous heritage or folklore should not automatically be treated as a source of public domain information. However, if a partnership mentality is adopted, which recognises the stewardship of indigenous peoples over their traditional and customary knowledge (especially in respect of natural resources and the environment), there may be a way forward. It could be that, on the condition of appropriate safeguards, many indigenous communities may be prepared to share aspects of their heritage which are in the nature of a global public good, particularly in the fields of biodiversity conservation and sustainable resource management.

The condition is that in allowing access to this knowledge, or by placing it in the public domain, there would need to be some means by which indigenous peoples could prevent the exploitation or inappropriate use of their heritage. This situation reflects the fact that some public domain information, even though it has been made publicly available, may still be subject to other constraints or interests.

There is an analogy between this situation and the copyleft movement. For example, the promoters of open source code use conventional laws (of contract and copyright) to constrain a subsequent developer, who may have enhanced the computer code, from trying to appropriate that knowledge in a way that excludes knowledge sharing. Until such time as indigenous peoples can establish a protective brand (such as an indigenous certification mark), or else entrench their indigenous heritage rights, their only protection is through the application of conventional IPR. Unfortunately, this is very limited protection because most indigenous knowledge does not satisfy the criteria for patent and copyright protection.

Despite the presumption that indigenous heritage should not be treated as public domain information, there is real potential for the information commons, through appropriate partnering arrangements which acknowledge indigenous primacy over the use of their own heritage and information. To illustrate, there is a collaborative initiative currently underway which is the first of its kind in Aotearoa New Zealand. This involves collaborative effort between a public Crown Research Institute (CRI), Industrial Research, and Victoria University and the Mother Aubert Home of Compassion Trust Board. The scientists from the Institute and the University are working with local Maori (the indigenous people) to return knowledge based on ancient Maori herbal remedies to the local indigenous people as the rightful holders of that information.

In 1897, a Catholic nun working with the indigenous peoples, Mother Suzanne Aubert, produced "Mother Aubert's Herbal Remedies". She used the knowledge passed on to her by indigenous Maori healers and herbalists. For some reason, she destroyed all these records, it is thought due to a concern that this knowledge should not fall into the wrong hands or be used inappropriately. The remedies are based on the use of native plants which have healing properties. Much of this ancient herbal knowledge has been lost to the local indigenous people for over 100 years. The scientists have entered into an agreement with the indigenous people to engage in reverse ethno-botany of the remnants of these herbal remedies in an attempt to return that knowledge. The scientists have agreed that they will not commercialise the remedies. They see the benefits as being the development of analytical tools as a by-product (which could have future commercial application), but more importantly the development of a model for other partnership arrangements with indigenous peoples.

The project has received public funding from the Public Good Science Fund. The main incentive for this collaborative effort is to set a precedent of partnering with the rightful guardians of this ancient knowledge and returning it to communal ownership. Whether it will then make its way into the wider public domain is unknown at this stage; that will be a decision for the indigenous custodians of the repatriated knowledge.

A significant amount of public domain information comprises information generated or made available by government. Public authorities hold information that could be considered to be "public content". For example, there are policy documents written by government departments, national archives and records, national registers. There are the minutes and records of meetings; there are ordinances and laws. Access to this information is very much dependent on each country's approach to governance, its ICT capacity and the degree to which its citizens have entered the e-world.

The barriers to accessing public content are numerous. In terms of governance, a critical obstacle is whether or not the country practices "open government", where there is a presumption of availability of official information entrenched in the law. There are the obvious economic obstacles of access fees or charges which discourage the retrieval of information, the lack of capacity in technological terms and in human terms and the failure to digitise print records or to set up systems which promote universal access.

Freedom of Information

Access to public domain information, such as public content, is consistent with support for democratic processes. A government which promotes access to public content is an open government and more likely to encourage greater participation by its citizens and to believe in the importance of transparency and accountability for decision-makers.

Over the past 25 years, many countries have enacted freedom of information legislation. These laws reverse the presumption of government secrecy in favour of a principle of availability. Information held by government can be accessed by its citizens on request. These laws reflect a balancing exercise. There are always other interests which justify the withholding of the information. This is the reason FOI laws contain exemptions to allow a government department to refuse to release requested information on the specific grounds set out in the law. Common reasons for withholding information are to protect the privacy of individuals, to protect a country's intelligence and national security secrets, to avoid prejudicing a criminal investigation, to enable advisers to give free and frank advice to their ministers.

The boundaries as to the availability of public content in the form of official information held by government, are quite subtle. There are an infinite variety of circumstances that could apply to the broad categories and exemptions set out in FOI laws. The model that has been adopted in many FOI laws has been to introduce the concept of an overriding public interest or public good test and to establish an independent office to be the arbiter of these decisions. At the same time, an effective model would avoid charges which are so high as to amount to a barrier to access by prohibiting ordinary citizens from accessing government information.

Public interest in disclosure

There is a wide range of social objectives underlying the provision of public content. At one end of the spectrum are the "public good" or "public interest" policy objectives. These involve circumstances where the public's welfare will be better served through access to or disclosure of information, rather than a paternalistic approach where decisions are made on behalf of the people without informing or consulting them.

Examples include making information available concerning health services where the health service provider, such as a laboratory or a hospital, has failed to provide diagnostic services or treatment at an adequate standard. Irrespective of the ownership or status of that service provider, citizens are entitled to access this information for a number of reasons, such as to enable them to avoid risks to their health, or to chose another provider or to apply pressure to rectify the failure.

The same reasoning applies to environmental concerns, or to the misuse of public funds and so on. This public interest in access to information is sometimes articulated in law or official policies, known as "whistleblowing". This form of protected disclosure regime can apply to both public and private sector organisations.

The amount of public content is also growing in response to what is known as consumer protection demands. The growth of consumer protection laws has had the effect of increasing the volume and categories of information in the public domain. There are now numerous reporting requirements in many countries on both private and public organisations which are designed to regulate certain behaviour or activities for the public good. This includes laws to ensure that consumers and shareholders have access to financial and market information to enable them to improve the quality of their decision-making. Another objective is to make it harder for agencies to monopolise information and in that way to disadvantage individuals or consumers.

The recognition of the importance of social capital is another social objective inherent in expanding the information commons. There are many social benefits to be derived from a more knowledgeable population. Public funding of libraries, archives, museums, educational institutions and research institutes are all manifestations of this recognition.

E-governance

Another major influence on the information commons is the growth in e-governance. In recent years, the growth in and significance of electronic commerce has prompted governments to consider their own leadership role in encouraging the efficiencies and economies of using electronic systems. The response has been a number of formal resolutions at international fora for governments to promote e-governance.

Specific action plans include the development of governmental communication systems, the use of e-procurement, and more significantly in terms of the growth of public domain information, digitising government held databases and records and then implementing online systems to facilitate their accessibility. Although many of these records and databases are in the public domain in print, their digitisation and online availability should result in more information of this nature becoming available over time.

These developments face the usual challenges of resourcing, the project difficulties inherent in implementing very large interconnected ICT systems, the attitudinal issues of a reluctance or inability of citizens to make use of these new delivery mechanisms, and a general lack of computer literacy. Of course, these obstacles are not just challenges but major impediments for developing countries.

National information policies

Governments have a critical leadership role in the quest to expand public domain information. The first challenge is attitudinal. Policy makers must have a willingness to consider the benefits of making public content available. This requires an appreciation of the implications of access to information for governance, for the development of social capital and for economic welfare.

There is a responsibility on governments to create the right information age environment, for example by adopting a national information policy which commits to a co-ordinated plan of action in each of the key areas of legislation, regulation, infrastructure development, exploitation of information, education, science and culture.

This keystone policy must recognise the importance of co-operation and horizontal networking. It should contain pilot projects, partnership proposals, and funding mechanisms to address the three key issues identified by librarian professionals as, "Connectivity (creating information networks, providing universal access, ensuring inter-operability); Content (creating core content for the public good, ensuring effective delivery of content, protecting citizens' rights, free access to core information); and Competencies (developing universal information literacy, supply of information specialists, information strategies for organisations)"

One measure which could be pursued by an appropriate international agency is to compile an inventory of pilot projects or models that have been established around the world and have a proven track record in achieving the balance between generating public domain information, which is universally accessible, while still satisfying some of the other objectives (such as financial returns, creation incentives or other form of benefit).

Many governments are at a critical stage in the development of their national information strategies. It would be very useful to have an information resource which could provide ideas on funding mechanisms and approaches to common problems and obstacles, especially where they face similar constraints, or are trying to establish an initiative in the same kind of conditions or ICT environment.

Immigration policies

There is good reason why knowledge creation is discussed in terms of "human capital". The key resource in the information age is people. Governments, by their control over immigration policy, are the gatekeepers to this resource. The cross-border flow of skilled migrants, or of hired foreign experts, has a significant effect on knowledge and technology transfer and indirectly on the growth of public domain information. The outflow of human capital from developing countries to industrial economies is currently a great source of concern. As a consequence, governments and business should address the social and economic incentives (including job opportunities, financial and tax incentives and social stability) to try to repatriate this knowledge. Other measures (eg. those adopted in China, India and Taiwan) include tapping into the expertise of overseas nationals for useful technical and market information (relayed to home-based producers) or to broker trade between home nationals and overseas business.

Research and development

Government initiatives, such as establishing public research centres and providing special fiscal incentives for research and development (R&D) which is properly focussed on the needs of the productive sector, can result in more information being placed in the public domain (as a condition of this assistance). This does not preclude the commercialisation of the outputs of research, but can ensure a more equitable access to this knowledge for other developers.

Some of the reform measures suggested by the World Bank to improve the quality and output of public R&D laboratories include corporatising these institutes to become true technology companies, capping the government contribution to their budgets, improving researchers' pay and recognition, providing other firms with direct incentives to place research contracts with the R&D institutes, and encouraging the assistance of foreign investors or strategic partners.

A more results oriented, market-based mode of operation, to increase the productivity of these R&D institutes, does not preclude a public domain charter which recognises the importance of universal access to knowledge creation. Although there would be constant tension in managing the balance between incentives and innovation, it is possible to structure the returns on investment so that the public funding in the R&D institute is akin to a government shareholding. This means that the returns are not necessarily made as financial dividends; under a pre-agreed charter there could be a recognition that a proportion of the institute's work and outputs must be made available to other researchers.

Role of public authorities

The role of public authorities in generating public content and building the capacity for countries to achieve universal access, is fundamental to their core responsibility. Rather than an "all or nothing" approach to the constant challenge of insufficient resources for public funding, there are many creative initiatives and models which have been implemented throughout the world; these demonstrate how the balance can be struck between ensuring the growth of and access to public domain information, while maintaining the necessary incentives and stimuli for knowledge creation. See the earlier suggestion for a specialised international inventory of significant examples. There is a growing recognition among public authorities that the interdependence of social and economic welfare means that the return on investment in developing public domain information has a value that goes beyond the financial returns. The partnering arrangement between the scientists and the local indigenous people, in respect of the repatriation of the ancient knowledge of Mother Aubert's herbal remedies, serves as an illustration of this hope for the future.

Citizen's Contribution to the Public Domain

The global developments to facilitate universal access to public domain information are only the beginning; they are laying essential groundwork for the global knowledge society. However, the potential benefits of these objectives will never be realised without the participation of the people. Rather than just becoming users of digital technologies, citizens must be encouraged and empowered to become content producers. The current level of development and capacity, even among industrialised countries, is still at the stage of building the framework of the knowledge society; it is like building a house where its intended residents are still a long way from being able to move in and enjoy what it will have to offer. The lack of human capacity, in terms of computer literacy and confidence, essential skills and education, training resources, and attitude, are proving fundamental barriers to the development of an inclusive knowledge society and to the participation of the very people it is hoped to benefit.

Political incentives

It is implicit in the previous discussion on the role of public authorities, that there is a clear link between open government and encouraging citizen involvement. The goal of FOI laws is to encourage participatory democracy. If citizens can access the information held by government, such as its policies and basis of decision-making, this would encourage more active participation in consultative and democratic processes. An informed population can contribute to debate, make the people's views known on issues and influence outcomes. These forces are a very powerful incentive for citizens to become content producers, for example as they start to communicate with each other to build a collective consciousness and to make their views known through the World Wide Web.

One of the challenges for governments and decision-makers, even in those countries which have adopted FOI legislation, is the unwillingness of these parties to accept the legitimacy of citizen empowerment and the subsequent anxiety created by the scrutiny and demands of citizens as they start to have more influence over the decision-making processes. These perceived threats are not just constrained to government, but also to those professional and other bodies who traditionally have enjoyed a position of power in society. For example, the Internet has provided the means for health consumers to challenge the historical monopoly wielded by health professionals over health information and service provision. Those who traditionally have controlled the dissemination of information will continue to resist this loss of domination. This resistance and the anxiety over the political consequences of empowering citizens, pose a significant challenge to universal access.

The entrenching of FOI governance models can both encourage and empower citizens to move beyond just their access rights to become participators and content producers as they make their influence felt. This is a significant motivation for citizens to contribute to the growth in public domain information.

E-literacy

In addition to the constraints of certain political systems on access and participation, there is a major obstacle to citizen contribution with the problems of e-literacy. In order for citizens to build their personal and ICT capacity to become content producers, they will require, in addition to the hardware and software at an affordable price, the confidence, skills and on-going support to be active participators.

One of the by-products of the efficiencies and economies that governments hope to achieve through the introduction of electronic government services, is a greater familiarity, confidence and skill-building among the citizens who use these online or other electronic systems. The transition from print to digital content will gradually bring about a far more sophisticated population in terms of its ability to use electronic information retrieval systems.

Attitudinal change

A key impediment to e-literacy is attitude. Citizens will not become content producers if they are not users of technology, such as the Internet. One of the current barriers to e-literacy is that even where people can afford to access ICT, they chose not to do so because they do not perceive that the content or the functionality is meaningful for them. It is obviously important to address these perceptions, however, there will not be a change in attitude unless these particular people or groups can be convinced as to the benefits of participating or using the Internet.

This may require the identification of target groups for special measures which can demonstrate the benefits and opportunities from upskilling and choosing to access and produce content, such as on the World Wide Web. An example might be with rural communities, where it is possible to demonstrate the importance of participation for regional development.

By using the technology to improve communication to share and obtain information and to improve social cohesiveness, it might be demonstrated that rural communities could become more effective in addressing internal problems and external constraints,

"The Internet is a powerful tool for rural dwellers to overcome many of the costs associated with networking and resource mobilisation - time, weather, transport difficulties and distance—and is an important network in its own right for accessing and sharing knowledge. The Internet also has the potential to help rural centres avert declines in population and even attract new residents by increasing access to higher education and business opportunities."

This attitudinal shift does not happen in isolation; it requires the support and targeted initiatives of government and other agencies to help particular groups in society or communities to understand the benefits of ICT and the significance of them becoming e-literate, as well as providing information on how to achieve this.

Tertiary education

Tertiary education is an integral requirement for e-literacy; it is a fundamental pre-requisite to the ability of citizens to participate in the production of and access to information; it develops a person's capability for learning, for interpreting information, and for adapting that knowledge to local conditions , all of which are critical factors in the uptake of ICT.

There are a number of emphases which are important in terms of directing education resources to the pre-requisites for an information-based society. The World Bank's studies on knowledge creation report that information-based technologies are more demanding in skills for diffusing, interpreting and applying knowledge. Besides teaching new and better skills, tertiary education and technical training produce people who can monitor technological trends, assess their relevance to the country's prospects, and help develop an appropriate national technological strategy. Countries at or near the technological frontier need strong tertiary education and research institutions to compete in the creation of new knowledge.

One of the issues which needs to be addressed is the use of patents by publicly funded research institutions, such as universities, to appropriate knowledge for the benefit of the institution. This is a significant source of funding for many seriously under-financed universities; if they are unable to benefit from patent claims, this could have disastrous financial repercussions. Any move to resist the patenting of university research must also address the funding issue and the negative impact on research projects if this source of funding were to be removed.

In one sense, what some might call public domain information (that is, the research from a public institution) is being applied to the benefit of the public (for a public good); the returns from the patented research are being applied as funding for the public institution. However, this patenting practice also "locks up" the knowledge produced by taxpayer funded researchers, with the result that this knowledge is excluded from the information commons.

Lifelong learning

Lifelong learning in ICT is essential to citizen participation, "With the growing complexity of knowledge, the speed with which it is being updated, and the sheer quantity of information to be interpreted, people today need to engage in structured and systematic learning throughout their lives."

The measures to achieve this include taking the technology to the people and increasing their confidence and familiarity with the use of ICT. This is an extension of the concept of mobile libraries and information booths. Communities should ensure that there are Internet outlets in places where people congregate, such as in community halls, churches, waiting rooms and shopping malls. Even the keyboard information displays in museums and galleries have a role to play in breeding familiarity.

Outreach

Another measure to facilitate contribution is to provide special support for initiatives which reach those communities or sectors of the population who up until now have been excluded from the loop. An example is the phenomenal growth in senior citizen Internet user groups. There is nothing to stop government and other stakeholders in an outreach programme from brokering partnering arrangements between equipment and service providers, negotiating discount arrangements, and generally facilitating connection on the basis that as the number of users grow, so do the returns both for the original financial investors and any other sponsor motivated by the social benefits of having facilitated ICT access and participation.

In considering what might encourage citizens to participate in information production, as opposed to mere access, we should not underestimate the role of civic duty and leisure. As well as political activity, we can expect voluntary associations and civic organisations to use the Internet and other ICT as a means of reaching their own members and a wider audience. As well as accessing information, there is great potential for the communication and exchange of ideas among these interest groups, much of which could become public domain information.

Technical support and mentoring

If citizens are to change from passive consumers of knowledge to active ICT participants in an information-based society, they need constant support, whether technical, upskilling or in the form of mentoring. This is vital if citizens are going to become serious content producers, because of the need for web page development skills, language translation services and other necessities. It is to be expected that there will be an outlet for the services of librarians and other intermediaries to fulfil this support function, and thereby play their part in facilitating the contribution of citizens to the growth of the information commons.

4

Reforms of the Public Sector

Public sector reform in India has consisted of five main components: increased efficiency, decentralisation, increased accountability, improved resource management, and marketisation. 'Information age reform' means delivering these ongoing reform components with a more overt role for information and with greater use of information technology. A review of global experience suggests that information age reform has great potential to improve public administration and other components of the public sector.

However, the Indian reality – like that for many developing countries – has been more problematic, with many failures of such reform; failures that can be described as total, partial or failures of sustainability and replication. The explanation for such failure lies partly in the approach to reform adopted by senior public officials. A 'four Is' model of approaches is described: the pre-information age approach of 'ignore', and the information age approaches of 'isolate', 'idolise' and 'integrate'. Analysis of Indian cases suggests it is the last approach that is most likely to deliver reform objectives; yet it remains the least commonly-adopted. Changes are therefore required in current strategies for public administration training and the management of change. Such findings will hold true for many other developing countries.

Public sector reform is, if generally defined, change within public sector organisations that seeks to improve their performance. As such, reform can be seen as an ongoing process in India since the inception several centuries ago of institutions that we now label 'public sector'. However, reform is typically defined more narrowly. It is often associated with the ideology of the 'New Right' towards the public sector; an ideology that grew up especially from the 1970s and which sought particular types of change in the way the public sector was run. This ideology has, albeit slowly and by 'fits and starts', increasingly begun to shape the agenda for change in the Indian public sector.

What constitutes the public sector reform agenda in India? There has been no consistent menu of elements but typical components – driven by the global agenda of new public management – include those listed below.

— *Increased efficiency*: improving the input:output ratio within the public sector. The rationale of such reforms is to address the large size of public sector expenditure and/or the inefficiency of many of its processes.

— *Decentralisation*: the transfer of decision making to lower, more localised levels of the public sector. The rationale of such reforms is to reduce the costs of centralised decision making, and to create more flexible and responsive decision making.

— *Increased accountability*: making public sector staff more accountable for their decisions and actions. The rationale of such reforms is to increase the pressure on staff to perform well, to make them more responsive to recipient groups, and to reduce inefficient or corrupt practices.

— *Improved resource management*: increasing the effective use of human, financial and other resources. The rationale of such reforms is clear from their definition. It often includes a refocusing of the way the performance of these resources is planned, measured and managed.

— *Marketisation*: increasing the use of market forces to cover relationships within the public sector, relationships between citizens ('consumers') and the public sector, and relationships and boundaries between public and private sector. The rationale of such reforms is that market relations will drive costs down and increase efficiency and/or effectiveness of service delivery.

There has been much criticism of the components listed: of what they seek to achieve in theory, and of what they do and do not achieve in practice.

Indian Realities of Information Age Reform

Almost simultaneous with the development of a reform agenda, there has been a growing sense in India of a real or impending 'information age'. The roots of ideas about a new 'information age' – treated here as synonymous with emergence of an 'information economy', 'information society' or 'post-industrial society' – are invariably traced back to the work of writers such as

Daniel Bell, Fritz Machlup, Yuji Masuda and Alvin Toffler. Through analysis of extant trends, they described a vision of a new world paradigm that was already coming into existence and that would increasingly develop. General features of this new paradigm include a domination of services over other economic sectors, niche instead of mass markets, and the emergence of a 'post-bureaucratic' form of organisation.

The early, and optimistic, writings about the information age have been much criticised. Critics argue:

— That things have not changed as much as predicted. Peasant farmers – who, with their families, form a major proportion of the world's population – continue to live and work much as they have ever done. They have yet to appreciate the pleasures of surfing the Net or teleworking. Even in the high citadels of the new world, shifts in working patterns and social life may be tangible and important, but they are not yet revolutionary. A modified criticism is therefore that change has been, and will be, a very uneven process that creates inequalities.

— That, when things do change, there will be problems as well as benefits. The information age may be marked by higher living standards but also by unemployment, insecurity, electronic surveillance and alienation.

— That the technology focus of information age writing distracts us from the human, social and political factors which explain – and therefore ultimately determine – what happens in our world.

There is a great deal of validity in these criticisms, but what they do not deny is that – albeit slowly and unevenly, for better or worse – there are identifiable information age trends. Thus, while the concept of an information age retains a large measure of hyperbole, it does serve to highlight important trends that are shaping the world in which we live.

It is certain that they have begun to shape the economic and political context in India. Whilst many see the 1970s as something of a 'lost decade' for India in computing terms, the country more than made up in the 1980s. The 1984—87 period in office of 'Rajiv and his computer boys' marked a defining moment during which India's image and activity as a global software player really began to take off, and during which a clear link was made between computing and reform of Indian public administration.

Although information technology (IT) has never since been so heavily-championed at such a high level in government, the catalytic actions of the mid-1980s set loose two specific, related and seemingly unstoppable information age trends in India:

- The increasing importance of information, including the increasing visibility and value of information systems.
- The increasing use of information technology.

Defining IT and IS

Information technology can be defined as computing and telecommunications technologies that provide automatic means of handling information. IT is therefore taken here to represent equipment: both the tangible hardware and the intangible software. A computer linked to other computers on a local area network represents one example of IT.

Information systems (IS) can be defined as systems of human and technical components that accept, store, process, output and transmit information. They may be based on any combination of human endeavours, paper-based methods and IT. A financial information system of staff and computers that gathers data and processes it into reports used for managerial decision making represents one example of an IS. Thus:

- IT on its own does not do anything useful; in order to do anything, it must become part of an information system.
- Information systems do not necessarily involve computers and telecommunications equipment.
- Even when they do, information systems are much more than just IT because they involve people and their actions.

For the public sector in India, this means that one can therefore see a trend of 'information age reform' that combines the existing reform agenda with the promise of the information age. Indeed, from humble beginnings in the Indian Statistical Institute in 1956, government expenditure on IT has grown to average more than US$350m per annum by the late 1990s.

Information age reform is therefore a growing reality for India which means two things that are different from traditional reform:

- A much greater role for information and information systems in the processes of change in the public sector.

— A much greater role for information technology in the processes of change in the public sector.

There is great potential for these trends of information age reform to bring significant benefits to India because government has been, and still remains, the single largest collector, user, holder and producer of information. Information is a central resource for all staff levels and for all activities: 'In pursuing the democratic/political processes, in managing resources, executing functions, measuring performance and in service delivery, information is the basic ingredient'.

The work of government is thus very information-intensive, and four main types of formal information are identifiable:

— *Information to support internal management*. This includes information about staff for personnel management, and information about budgets and accounts for financial management. Like the other three types of information, it can be used for everything from day-to-day operational implementation up to long-term policy analysis and planning.

Information to support public administration and regulation. This includes information that records the details of the main 'entities' in India: people, business enterprises, buildings, land plots, imports/exports, etc. It is used for a variety of purposes such as legal, judicial and fiscal.

— *Information to support public services*. Examples include education, health (e.g. patient records), transport (e.g. passenger reservation information) and public utilities (e.g. customer billing information).

— *Information made publicly available.* This includes:

— Information government wishes to disseminate such as press releases, consultation papers, details of policies, laws and regulations, and details of benefits and entitlements.

— Information government collects that it may make available, such as demographic or economic statistics.

— Information government is required to supply such as audited accounts, internal policy documents and correspondence, and responses to requests from politicians or journalists or citizens.

Given this information-intensity, changes in information systems must be an essential part of all reform initiatives in India, and changes in information technology will also have a great potential.

In theory, everything that IT can do could be done by some other means. In practice, its ability to increase the speed and/or reduce the cost of information tasks mean it can do things that would not otherwise be contemplated. IT therefore can bring change and has three basic change potentials within reform:

— *Supplant*: automate existing human-executed processes which involve accepting, storing, processing, outputting or transmitting information. For example, the automation of existing clerical functions.

— *Support*: assist existing human-executed processes. For example, assisting existing processes of government decision making, communication, and decision implementation.

— *Innovate*: create new IT-executed processes or support new human-executed processes. For example, creating new methods of public service delivery.

IT can bring five main benefits to the reform process. In practice, these are not neatly differentiated but they can be summarised as:

— *Cheaper*: producing the same outputs at lower total cost.

— *More*: producing more outputs at the same total cost.

— *Quicker*: producing the same outputs at the same total cost in less time.

— *Better*: producing the same outputs at the same total cost in the same time, but to a higher quality standard.

— *For the first time*: producing new outputs.

The first three represent efficiency gains for the public sector; the last two represent effectiveness gains. Of course, these are the direct and objective benefits. IT can bring many others such as better staff motivation, greater political control, or an improved public image for the organisation (with Indian Railways being a case in point for all three of these indirect benefits).

IT is therefore seen to have a great potential to contribute to reform, with this potential being illustrated by the following examples from around the world:

— *Increased efficiency*: IT's role in increasing efficiency has been described above, mainly relating to its 'supplant' role. In the US, the Lawrence Livermore National Laboratory developed a World Wide Web-based system to reduce the cost and increase the speed of parts procurement.

— *Decentralisation*: IT can provide support for more efficient and effective decision making at decentralised locations and create new information flows that incorporate those locations. In Ireland, the Department of Social Welfare created more than a dozen computerised applications in order to support the decentralisation of responsibilities from Dublin to outlying offices.

— *Increased accountability*. IT can create new accountability information and can deliver accountability information to new recipients, providing for more efficient or effective accountability. In the US, 'collusion detection software' was developed and applied to root out impropriety in bids and contract awards for supply of public school milk.

— *Improved resource management*: IT can create new performance information and deliver it to decision makers, providing more effective managerial control over government resources. In Malaysia, government development authorities collaborated to develop a computerised system to facilitate land resource management.

— *Marketisation*. IT can supply the new information necessary for the establishment of market relations, and can also form the conduit for delivery of new forms of public service. 'In Spain and Portugal, smart cards are issued to people to claim unemployment benefit at kiosks, and to check on job vacancies and training opportunities.'

Globally, then, new information systems and new information technology are both supporting and driving forward the process of public sector reform. But what of India? Has the country unleashed the power of information age reform, or does the potential still lie mainly dormant?

Objective reporting of information age reform cases in India (and elsewhere) is rare. Many reports are written from a 'rose-tinted' viewpoint by those with a vested interested in the reform initiative. Their glowing and uncritical claims of success frequently bear little relation to reality. Nonetheless, reliable cases can be found and one can place these into three categories.

Computerisation of the Indian Railways' Passenger Reservation System may be branded a success. Not only did it significantly increase the efficiency of the reservation process, but it also reduced corruption (though did not eliminate it), increased rail staff morale, and improved the quality of customer service. Beyond these reform components, it also gave Indian Railways a more modern image, and it helped to build information age capabilities within the country. Sadly, this case remains almost a lone beacon in India which 'seems to stand out as a solitary example of success.'

A few ongoing information age reform projects have yet to fall clearly into the categories of either success or failure. Perhaps the best-known of these is CRISP, the Computerised Rural Information Systems Project. When initially analysed, after some five years of operation, this appeared to have made little impact and to be heading for failure. Subsequent analysis, however, revealed 'sparks of life' within the project, with some computers being used to support analytical management decision making, thereby enabling decentralisation and improved delivery of assistance.

By far the largest category of reports – both from the formal literature and from the dozens of Indian public servants trained each year by the author – is that of failure. There are no cast-iron statistics on this and there are unlikely ever to be. Nonetheless, based on the available evidence, one can state with some degree of certainty that the majority of information age reform initiatives in India end in failure.

This may be the *total failure* of an initiative never implemented or in which a new system is implemented but immediately abandoned; the *partial failure* of an initiative in which major goals are unattained or in which there are significant undesirable outcomes; the *sustainability failure* of an initiative that succeeds initially but then fails after a year or so; or the *replication failure* of an initiative that succeeds in one place but cannot be repeated elsewhere.

Formally-reported examples include the following:

— The Director of Adult Education in the National Literacy Mission Authority was smitten by the potential of IT to improve the management of literacy programmes. Having seen a software firm's demonstration, and despite glaring technical and data constraints that were obvious to any neutral observer, he commissioned a complex executive information system (EIS) that soon fell squarely into the 'total failure' category.

— Part of the Income Tax Department's tax system was computerised. The project ran into difficulties due to political antagonisms between various groups;

notably between regional tax commissioners and the central tax board, and between management and unions. As a result, only parts of the information system and only a sub-set of intended process reforms became operational and even these were resisted by staff. There was therefore only very limited achievement of reform objectives.

— A computerised decision support system (DSS) was created for the Narmada Irrigation Project Authority. The system was initially used to increase efficiency by helping engineers save time in their cost estimations of canal engineering work. However, the system was never properly used for its main intended purpose: the production of improved canal design. Upon retirement of the Chief Engineer who had championed use of the DSS, even the estimation use was discontinued.

— A computerised management information system was developed in Surendranagar district, Gujarat state, to demonstrate the feasibility of providing computer support to planning and monitoring tasks at the district level, thereby enabling decentralisation. Although the system proved useful, it was never adopted elsewhere because other district officers had a 'not invented here' mentality that rejected innovations made by anyone other than themselves.

One is naturally drawn to analyse why failure should be so prevalent in India. There are almost as many explanations for failure as there are information systems. However, one key factor that emerges again and again from case study analysis is the attitude and actions of senior public officials, both politicians and managers. Based on discussions with such officials and their subordinates, and a review of relevant cases, we can create a 'four Is' model of different approaches to information age reform that appear over time, as described below.

The 'Ignore' Approach: In this case, public officials are ignorant about IT and information systems. They therefore do not include consideration of either in their plans for reform. IT expenditure is minimal or non-existent. This approach does not constitute information age reform and will therefore not form a major focus of this chapter. Nevertheless, this approach is still found in many – perhaps even most – Indian public sector organisations. This is sometimes even so when computers are present for, in some cases, those computers remain unused and merely act as costly 'executive paperweights'.

The 'Isolate' Approach : In this approach, public officials remain computer-illiterate and lack an understanding of information's role. They nevertheless are aware of IT and its potential. Investment in IT is therefore included in reform plans but is seen as the separate responsibility of 'computer experts'. It is mainly associated with automation and some (often spurious or concocted) idea that efficiency gains will result. For other reform agendas, it is added as an afterthought and is not linked in any systematic way to the process of reform. This, nonetheless, represents the first step on the path of information age reform.

Both the early years of the CRISP project and the Indian Income Tax project cited above are examples of the isolate approach. In these cases, the introduction of computers was seen as the responsibility of technical staff rather than being something in which mainstream managers should become involved. As a result, huge investments made very little, if any, contribution to reform agendas in these Indian public sector organisations.

This approach should not be seen as some historical aberration for it can still be found. The recent Asian Development Bank-supported project for restructuring of Gujarat's financial sector provides an example:

'Yet when it comes to computerisation, the cart has been put before the horse. There is a separate allocation for computerisation ... The type of hardware and its allocation to various tax collection agencies has already been decided. It was envisaged that the process of computerisation would be completed even before the thinking on financial sector reform made any headway.'

The 'Idolise' Approach: In this approach, public officials have become semi-literate. They use computers and are over-aware of IT's potential. They believe that IT can transform the business of government (or at least transform their own career/political prospects if they are seen to initiate a high-profile IT project). They are dimly aware that information is something important. The public sector becomes awash with IT-driven reform projects which place technology at the heart of the change process.

This approach has recently leapt to prominence thanks to N. Chandrababu Naidu, Chief Minister of Andhra Pradesh state. In 1997, he launched a high-profile project – the LEAP21 (Leadership and Excellence in Andhra Pradesh in the twenty-first century) initiative – that exactly fits the idolise description. This initiative aims to use IT as a main lever in the creation of better government in Andhra Pradesh and, more generally, 'focuses ... on using Information Technology as a strategic tool for improving the quality of life for the people of Andhra Pradesh.'

The jury currently remains out on LEAP21. Chief Minister Naidu's intention of using state promotional interventions to support the development of the IT industry and IT technological capabilities is based on sound historical precedent. However, his hopes of driving public sector reform with IT are not. There is a long history of failure to deliver reform objectives via technology-driven projects, of which the literacy EIS case cited above is but one example.

Even where technology-centred projects initially appear to succeed in delivering reform objectives, Bhatnagar warns that they may not be sustainable or replicable since they so often depend on a single 'idolising' figurehead. When that senior official transfers to a new post, the project often collapses; when other organisations try to copy, failure ensues because the originator's drive or skills are lacking; and copying rarely takes place because 'a replication will never attract the same attention as a first time use'. In all situations, the cause is the lack of the original IT-focused champion.

Examples of these sustainability and replication failures from India include the canal design and district administration cases cited above, and another DSS used to support improved planning of resource usage in two zonal railways which was never used in other zones. With LEAP21 so focused on Naidu himself, prospects are limited for the sustainability and replication of any successes it may fortuitously achieve.

The 'Integrate' Approach: In this approach, public officials have become information-literate. They recognise information as a key organisational resource that is central to all government functions. IT is relegated to a secondary role: it is seen as a valuable means to achieve certain reform ends, not as an end in itself. The reengineering of information systems and the introduction of IT are now fully integrated into the process of organisational change, driven by reform objectives.

The integrated approach therefore places information in the driving seat, relegating technology to an important but enabling role. In very simple terms, we can see four main steps in initiation of this approach:

- Acceptance by key stakeholders of the need for reform.
- Identification and communication of an agenda for reform.
- Identification of the new and/or reengineered information systems requirements of this reform agenda.
- Identification of the role, if any, that information technology has to play in meeting these requirements.

The successful computerisation of passenger reservations on Indian Railways can be seen to have followed this route. The need for reform of reservations was understood since at least the mid-1970s, with an agenda of modernisation widely discussed and the need for reengineering of systems to escape the old 'one-train-per-clerk' situation widely accepted. Information technology was then identified as the servant of this pre-existing reform agenda, not as the master of reform. Despite undeniable hiccups, this project was kept on track thanks to a vision of efficiency, accountability and customer service objectives that was shared by key stakeholders, not held by just one champion. As a result, technology solutions were shaped to fit reform objectives rather than vice versa, as is so often the case in examples of the idolise approach.

However, other examples of the integrated approach hardly exist in India. Approaches and chronologies remain unevenly distributed in India, but Bhatnagar sees much of the public sector still struggling to move away from the ignore stage. If anything, it seems likely to move on to 'idolise', as exemplified by the LEAP21 initiative, rather than 'integrate'.

Information age reform is seen as a relatively new activity in the Indian public sector that recognises a significant – at times even central – role for information systems and information technology. Information systems change has always been an essential part of all organisational change in government (though this may not have been well recognised at times). But what is palpably new in information age reform is the presence of information technology, which has been seen to have great potential to contribute to the reform process. Public officials are central to information age reform and they can take different approaches in trying to realise the potential of information and IT

Despite the potential of information age reform, there remain substantial problems a) for the Indian public sector to enter the information age reform era at all; and b) for it to move on within that era to an integrated approach that will use IT to effectively enable delivery of reform objectives.

There is no magic recipe for ensuring widespread use of the integrated approach but education and training must surely form a substantial part of the package. Yet any review of current public administration training programmes in India will show that most can be described as 'ignore going on idolise' in their approach. There is little attempt to build the hybrid managers – spanning managerial, IT and IS skills – that information age government requires (Mundy, forthcoming). These skill sets remain unintegrated within current training and often ignored. Some potential public employees and in-service trainees may gain computing skills on their training programmes, but they do not gain information or information systems knowledge and skills. Any view of IT beyond the hands-on is typically simplistically-positive.

Not only does this hamper integrated approaches today, it also hints at a dangerously self-reinforcing spiral. If the present generation of Indian public managers cannot value or manage information, that sets the 'information-blind' agenda for current training and debate, thus ensuring that the next generation, too, will be unable to value or manage information. A similar spiral runs the risk of developing a 'blinded by computers' agenda of IT idolatry.

Indian public managers will also need to adopt a more strategic approach to change that drives technology needs from information needs, and information needs from reform objectives. Strategic information systems planning of this type is very much in vogue in the private sector, though the application of such techniques in practice and in the public sector remains questionable (Ballantine and Cunningham, forthcoming). Perhaps more realistic is a 'core-periphery' approach that balances strategic and tactical, central and local needs.

Finally, encouraging an integrated approach will require cultural and structural changes in the Indian public sector to ensure that technology is the servant of reform. Such changes are never quick and so the move to an integrated approach can only be seen as a long-term process. In the interim, such information age reform initiatives as do take place in India are likely to remain dominated by isolate and, increasingly, idolise approaches. The true potential of information technology will therefore remain untapped in most cases, with initiatives undershooting in their delivery of reform objectives.

5

Public Domain Information

The importance of encouraging private sector contributions of public domain information cannot be underestimated. The trend over the past decade has been the increasing privatisation of research. Government fiscal pressure has resulted in the proportion of public funding for science and technology research and development to fall throughout the world. This has been replaced by more private sector involvement, resulting in greater reliance on patenting. For example, the Human Development Report 1999 cites that the portion of public sector patents in biotechnology sold under exclusive licence to the private sector rose from just 6% in 1981 to more than 40% by 1990.

The 1990s have also seen a boom in the number and value of mergers and acquisitions (especially in the biotechnology, telecommunications and computing industries), due to the increasing privatisation of research and rising costs for risky innovations. One of the recurring themes in the previous discussion is the delicate balance between the effect of incentives on knowledge creation and expanding and accessing public domain information. Without the appropriate incentives, whether financial or in some other form, the risk is that the knowledge creation process will be stymied. This needs to be borne in mind in any discussion on how the private sector can be encouraged to contribute to the information commons.

The measures to achieve private sector participation must be focussed on the returns, but in a way which recognises that returns on investment can take many forms. For example, in respect of any programme which is aimed at generating information which is a global public good, or facilitating universal access (whether in the national or international context), it may be worthwhile exploring measures such as:

— 'Tax incentives for participating in a partnering programme identified under the Action Plan of the country's National Information Policy.

— 'Subsidies or other assistance for properly targeted R&D, with formal agreements on how the knowledge may subsequently be commercialised and what must be put into the public domain.

— 'Knowledge transfer and skill building, by leasing private sector specialist personnel to a development project, so that the returns are the benefit of the expertise built up during the secondment period.

In order to achieve the right balance between the competing interests in each of the above suggestions, it is necessary to resolve the following issue in respect of each project or public funding proposal; at what point in the development cycle is it possible to redistribute the knowledge gained from these processes to those who need it most, without seriously undermining the incentive system which is fundamental to stimulating large-scale investment in research programmes and to producing technological breakthroughs?

Any strategy to encourage private sector contribution should include lobbying on the significance of the public bargain implicit in the fair use doctrine. Much information of value which is generated in the private sector is subject to copyright, therefore it is extremely important to retain the fair use exception in copyright law as this is a significant source of public domain information.

The processes inherent in the knowledge society, particularly the empowerment of citizens, results in a more vocal and demanding environment not just for public authorities but also for the private sector. This is most apparent in the area of consumer protection, health, the environment, safety and basic rights.

As citizens become more computer literate and knowledgeable, their expectations will rise in respect of the information demands placed on business and industry. It is expected that, in response to consumer demands, the private sector will contribute to the growth of public domain information through the dissemination of information: about its policies, procedures or processes; what it has to offer in terms of marketing its goods and services; consumer rights and protections (for example, complaints procedures and other mandatory disclosure requirements); contractual terms and conditions; and, other forms of information deemed relevant to the relationship between a company and its consumers, not just by the company but by its citizens.

One development on the issue of private sector contributions to the information commons, but which is not without significant difficulties, is the mechanism of contingent lending. For example, the World Bank and other development institutions are investigating a new financing mechanism for AIDs research, known as a contingent loan. These types of loans recognise the scale of the contribution that private sector developers can make (in terms of having the requisite resources), but also the need to work within existing incentives paradigms.

The advantages of such a mechanism are described by the World Bank as follows, "The use of contingent lending might reduce uncertainty about projections of the price and quantity of future vaccine sales in developing countries, while leaving key product R&D in the hands of the private pharmaceutical firms (which are the entities with the resources and expertise to undertake this type of research). Under a contingent loan scheme, the international community would make binding commitments to lend to developing countries sufficient funds to buy large amounts of an AIDs vaccine, once such a vaccine has been invented and demonstrated safe and effective. By assuring the pharmaceutical firms of a future market, the scheme would reduce the risks to which those firms are exposed, giving them a stronger incentive to conduct the necessary research."

Another suggestion in the Human Development Report 1999 is the establishment of a representative group of independent scientists to identify critically important technological challenges which, if solved, would substantially improve the human development of the world's poorest people and address other global challenges to human security. The suggestion is that every five years the group could offer financial incentives and public recognition to researchers, public and private alike, for innovations that would be used in the global public interest. The Report suggests that funding of such initiatives could be by a levy on patents registered under the World Intellectual Property Organisation. As an alternative, it suggests that funding could be reallocated from research subsidies, grants and tax breaks which are currently provided to industry.

The dilemma is that in respect of the many significant and promising technological advances for human development, public institutions cannot afford and do not have the resources to carry out the research and development, whereas the private sector can only do so if the incentive structure is effective. The future may be in collaborative efforts, "Innovative policies are needed to ensure that much needed solutions for human development are pursued. Incentives are needed to turn research towards the pressing needs of the world, not just of those who pay."

Potential of digital technologies

Despite the great advances that have been made (such as through the advent of telecommunications), and despite the potential of digital technologies to bring about harmonisation effects and to facilitate collaboration, serious global imbalances persist. At a community level, addressing the digital divide is imperative for reasons of economic inclusion and social cohesiveness. In global terms, the polarisation effect of ICT and its exclusivity has been described as creating parallels worlds, "Those with income, education and - literally - connections have cheap and instantaneous access to information. The rest are left with uncertain, slow and costly access. When people in these two worlds live and compete side-by-side, the advantage of being connected will overpower the marginal and impoverished, cutting off their voices and concerns from the global conversation".

The previous discussions (for example on citizen access to and participation in the knowledge society, on the pre-requisites of e-literacy, and on knowledge as a global public good) are all applicable to developing countries and disadvantaged communities. The purpose of this section is to focus more sharply on the special needs and problems of these stakeholders and to identify potential measures to improve their access to public domain information.

The gap between the information rich and information poor has ominous implications in terms of its marginalising effect and the emergence of an "information underclass". What special measures are required to ensure that the deployment of ICT will meet the basic economic, social, political and cultural needs of all citizens, regardless of their ability to pay or where they live? More particularly, if universal access to public domain information is a foundation stone in building a global knowledge society, what special measures are required to ensure the development of and access to this information?

In terms of high level policies, the dilemma for developing countries and for very poor and disadvantaged communities is that they lack the basic utilities and fundamentals of human existence. It is difficult for the citizens of such countries and communities to appreciate the relevance of accessing public domain information if they still lack clean water, sanitation and vaccines. As well as lacking health and educational resources, there is a lack of suitable infrastructure (in the form of power supplies, telecommunications, and the appropriate operating environment and climatic conditions for computers and their networks).

The World Bank has identified three critical steps that developing countries must take to narrow knowledge gaps. These are:

— "Acquiring knowledge, which involves tapping and adapting knowledge available elsewhere in the world —for example, through an open trading regime, foreign investment, and licensing agreements - as well as creating knowledge locally through research and development, and building on indigenous knowledge.

— Absorbing knowledge, which involves, for example, ensuring universal basic education, with special emphasis on extending education to girls and other traditionally disadvantaged groups; creating opportunities for lifelong learning; and supporting tertiary education, especially in science and engineering.

— Communicating knowledge, which involves taking advantage of new information and communications technology - through increased competition, private sector provision, and appropriate regulation - and ensuring that the poor have access."

For those countries that are in a position to develop a National Information Policy, with specific action plans, there are a number of relevant themes and models which could feature in their information strategy. The following list illustrates the range of measures which could be considered to benefit both developing countries and disadvantaged communities:

ICT and Education

Continued investment in education and in building human capacity is fundamental. As well as addressing basic educational needs and literacy, the measures should focus on issues wider than just classroom use and connections. Teacher training in ICT is essential, particularly in schools serving low income communities because these students are less likely to have access to home computers or to have the resources for technological support. As well as training, there is a need for ongoing ICT support and mentoring.

Distance learning initiatives

There are many example of distance education, whether in the form of open universities or virtual classrooms. The African Virtual University is one such example. There has been much written about the pre-requisites for successful distance learning, including the need for connectivity and interoperability, equipment, properly tailored course content, and technical support to help students use and get the best out of their network.

Community Access Programmes

Examples include the advent of telecentres in developing

countries, and specific programmes in industrialised countries with targets to establish public access sites in remote and disadvantaged urban communities.

Networked information

For example, HealthNet supports healthcare workers in more than 30 developing countries by providing summaries of latest medical research, e-mail connectivity and access to medical libraries. It also supports a moderated, free e-mail list (ProMed) for the reporting of and requesting assistance on outbreaks of emerging infectious diseases. HealthNet uses radio and telephone-based computer networks and a low-earth-orbit satellite. It provides slower but cheaper access than the Internet and is accessible in areas with no telecommunications infrastructure.

Compromises in technology

The optimum capacity and speed in ICT should not be a pre-requisite to connectivity. For example, access need not be real time, particularly if a developing country or project sponsors can negotiate lower rates for using satellite down time. Other examples include the use of reconditioned second-hand computers. There are projects which use free-standing, solar powered computers which are updated daily with information relayed through radio handsets and cell phones from a regional centre with direct Internet access. The village computer acts as a bulletin board for the availability of information on medicines, credit, market prices, transport services, warnings of pest, weather and water risks, and provides educational material.

Leapfrogging

Developing countries do not have to experience all the various stages of ICT development as has been the case with most industrialised countries. Developing countries can take advantage of the time lag in technology developments to leapfrog technology. Examples are moving straight from under developed networks to fully digitised networks, bypassing the traditional analogue technology that is in use in most industrial countries. Developing countries can take advantage of new wireless technologies that require less fixed investment than traditional wire-based telecommunications and which can be more cost effective in countries with sparse populations, difficult terrain and harsh climatic conditions as they require less maintenance. Therefore, rather than relying on fixed telephone lines, under leapfrog technology the user may be able to obtain a cellular phone instead.

Leverage

The use of collective bargaining power based on a regional approach or shared interests, where countries or communities form a united negotiating block, can result in connectivity arrangements and discounting which would not otherwise be available through bilateral negotiations with service providers.

Advocacy

Developing countries must seize opportunities to make their presence felt and have their needs taken into account in negotiations on any review of the TRIPS

Agreement, and in the international debates over governance of the Internet (including over the allocation of domain names, proposals to tax electronic commerce and privacy developments).

Community focus

An important principle is the need to focus on group or community access, rather than individual or household ownership of ICT. The structures for enabling access (including the location and management of terminals and telecentres) must reflect the structures within the local community and the ways in which people prefer to congregate. The pilot Technology Access Community Centres (TACC) established in Egypt act as hubs for skills training and capacity building. Depending on the community, and any cultural constraints, access to ICT needs to be provided in places where people feel comfortable congregating. In respect of disadvantaged communities, such as low income neighbourhoods, public access sites can be situated in a variety of locations, ranging from the local tavern to state housing complexes.

Local content

Displaying local news, culture and other information relevant to the local community not only builds human capacity but demonstrates the relevance of ICT to the daily lives of those whom it can benefit most. In Canada, funding is provided under the Youth Employment Strategy to give young people experience in creating web sites featuring Canada's information resources. This is a type of "brokerage" arrangement where firms and other organisations are awarded contracts to hire young people to digitise their texts. There are other similar initiatives in respect of aboriginal and indigenous schemes to encourage the creation of content and the design of web sites.

Local leadership

The successful implementation of ICT relies on finding leadership and support from within the community, rather than this being imposed from the outside or top down from government. The Benton Report observes that efforts to encourage the spread of ICT in low income communities stand little chance of achieving lasting success unless they are firmly rooted in the community's own sense of their goals and needs. This emphasises the importance of nurturing individuals and indigenous community organisations that are already playing a helping role in the community, rather than trying to impose technology from the outside. This recognition involves identifying and working with recognised community leaders on ICT projects.

Telecommunications competition

Opening up a country's market to competing telecommunications and Internet service providers has resulted in significant increases in connectivity.

There will be other needs which must be protected in a competitive market, to ensure the benefits can reach all customers, such as those in rural or remote areas and not just those users who are located in the more lucrative urban areas. The radical changes in telecommunications markets, with the introduction of competition and new technologies, means that there is currently huge debate over the future of universal service and as to what form of regulation can best achieve this objective.

There are a number of ways that governments can provide incentives to encourage either the use or ownership of certain types of technologies. Examples include: eliminating tariffs and taxes on personal computers to encourage ownership; tax incentives to those businesses who supply equipment and ICT training to their employees; allowing employees to be able to borrow computers from their employers as a tax free benefit; significant discounting of course fees to encourage adults to enrol in training programmes to improve their basic computer literacy; start-up funding for individuals and small businesses to enable them to access ICT training; requiring a fixed number of free places for people who are unemployed, on benefits, on a low income, have disabilities, or are single parents, to enable them to attend introductory ICT courses; and specific opportunities for low income people to lease computers and software and to be provided with connectivity and advanced online and offline learner support.

It is important to take advantage of opportunities for developing countries (and communities) to consult and co-operate where they face similar challenges. In respect of resource intensive activities, it may be possible to achieve economies of scale, such as for ICT training of teachers, the development of support personnel, etc. A key issue for collaboration is the interoperability of networks and systems.Most recommendations on addressing the digital divide emphasise the importance of exploring partnerships among governments, industry, service providers, communities and interest groups. This is particularly important for the funding of research. There are other implications, such as illustrated by the numerous partnering arrangements set out in the Information Strategies of Australia, Canada and the United Kingdom.

An example is VolNet, which is a joint undertaking by the Canadian Federal Government and private and voluntary sectors. Under the administration of Industry Canada and the guidance of a National Advisory Committee (comprising private and voluntary sector representatives and Federal Officials), VolNet is seen as a model for providing structured support to the community and voluntary sector. It comprises a network of VolNet delivery agencies to provide services to eligible charitable and not-for-profit organisations. Through the partnership arrangements inherent in VolNet, it has been made possible to offer Internet connectivity (including equipment, skills development and support) to thousands of voluntary organisations.

Universal access, through formal training and support (such as in schools and libraries) is proving insufficient to overcome the ambivalence of many community groups to the uptake and relevance of ICT. As a consequence, the dissemination of technology must be through traditional and socially recognised learning channels. Many groups tend not to take advantage of formal avenues of training (such as provided by classrooms and libraries), but learn best from their peers (including friends and family). An adjunct to this requirement is the need to adapt public domain information to a form and manner that can be used by those whom it is intended to benefit.

Building trust is a priority because enabling access to information is of little long term benefit if people do not trust its source. This makes it essential to understand and listen to the needs and concerns of those who are the target of ICT assistance. It is essential to involve the beneficiaries of ICT projects in their design and implementation. When obtaining data on information and access needs, it is also important to ensure quantitative techniques are complemented by qualitative methods.

Producing local knowledge, and adapting existing public domain information to local conditions, is essential. This emphasises the need to inject public funding into local research. The World Bank sees adaptation as crucial, because for knowledge to be effective, it needs to be locally created or recreated, domestically "owned", and internalised. The World Bank Report notes that good principles must always be adapted to new circumstances, with domestic stakeholders (governments, businesses and citizens) taking the lead. Effective adaptation requires that governments and donors elicit and really listen to feedback from those whom the project is supposed to benefit.

There is a need for strong activism at the local and regional levels to ensure local communities have a voice in making their needs known to government, to service providers, and to other agencies, who have control over ICT and funding resources. Technology activists are necessary to lobby for local ICT training and educative initiatives to foster small business and regional and community development. As the Benton Report comments, "In the absence of strong grass roots pressure, telecommunications providers appear unlikely to deploy new technologies to low income communities voluntarily any time soon."

Role of international agencies

International agencies have a vital role to play in the provision of information as a global public good, particularly for the benefit of developing countries. This role can include the sponsorship of research where there are large social returns or benefits (which exceed private returns), but there have been insufficient incentives for any one company or country to invest in the research. The World Bank Report notes that many types of knowledge fall into the category of a national public good, but no single country will invest enough in the creation of such goods because the benefits would accrue to all countries without the creating country receiving full compensation. However, the Report notes that international institutions, acting on behalf of everyone, can fill this gap. It cites the example of the Consultative Group for International Agriculture Research.

The other role for international agencies is that of the intermediary. As the World Bank Report points out, the most important knowledge for development comes from developing countries and that it is this local knowledge creation, particularly its transfer between countries, which has the potential to unleash powerful development forces. It notes that each change in policy, and each development in a project, produces information that could be of benefit to another country. However, amassing that knowledge, assessing it and then sharing it with other countries is a task beyond the capacity (and self interest) of any single country. This provides a vital role for international agencies to support developing countries (and in some circumstances, at the community level) to innovate, adapt and evaluate projects, to assess policy changes and outcomes, and to build local capacity for policy analysis and evaluation.

Funding initiatives

A number of the measures discussed above include funding initiatives:

— 'There is the concept of contingent loans to fund the development of certain types of knowledge as a global public good.

— There is the proposal for a levy on patent applications filed with WIPO.

— The partnering arrangements, discussed in the context of private sector contribution to the information commons and R & D research projects, involve a mix of funding initiatives, such as allowing a certain level of commercialisation provided a significant amount of the research output is placed into the public domain.

Public funding initiatives can take many different forms. Some of the ideas which have been floated in the United States and elsewhere are as follows:

— Establishing a fund to make loans (among other objectives) to stimulate new technology development. An example is the Telecommunications Development Fund (USA) which apparently operates as a non-profit corporation and is capitalised with interest earned on money raised from spectrum auctions. One of the intentions of the Fund was to support universal service and to promote the delivery of telecommunications services to under served rural and urban areas.

— Assistance Programmes which can award grants for projects aimed at helping non-profit hospitals, tribal and local governments, libraries, schools, and community centres to use information technologies. These Programmes may include a concept of matching funds so that for every dollar obtained by grant, the applicant must raise either a percentage or an equivalent amount.

— Penalties awarded by telecommunications regulators (such as US State Regulatory Commissions) can be applied as a source of funding for technology initiatives which are in the public interest (for example, telecommunications education trust funds which finance research and education programmes aimed at minority and low income communities).

— Another funding initiative, similar in concept to the idea of a patent levy, is the concept of a "Bit tax". This proposal would impose a very small tax on the amount of data sent through the Internet, so that the cost for most users would be negligible, whereas the cumulative amount raised would be significant. This fund could be applied to the development of and facilitating access to information which is a global public good. The feasibility of such a proposal, let alone its logistics, is dubious, particularly given the inability to control cross-border Internet transactions. If these were amenable to taxation, it is likely that (despite the current debate over the pros and cons of e-commerce taxation) the means would already have been found to implement a "Bit tax", but for domestic objectives rather than those of global public good. However, there are other taxation proposals which merit further consideration.

The impact of globalisation is such that proposals to impose a global tax are not nearly as far fetched as they might have seemed a decade ago. There has been growing interest in such mechanisms, with an early proposal by economist James Tobin (in 1978) for a tax on foreign exchange transactions to be applied uniformly by all major countries, to deter speculation on currency fluctuation (known as a "Tobin Tax"). This initiative grew out of a shared concern among governments at the perceived irrational activities in global financial markets which can have a significant adverse impact on national economies . Another development along similar lines was the proposal tabled at the International Monetary Fund (IMF) in May 1998 to create a World Taxing Organisation, with the power to levy a global tax on international financial transactions and to orient the taxing policy of countries. Proposals such as the Tobin Tax provide an interesting analogy when considering the funding and incentive problems of addressing the digital divide and the global information commons.

The purpose of a global "digital tax" would be to facilitate the development of, and access to, information which is a global public good; for example, it could provide funding for research (or for the purchase of intellectual property rights) where there are significant social returns or benefits but insufficient incentives for any one company or country to invest in the research or to acquire the rights to that knowledge. As well as knowledge creation, the tax could also fund specific measures within developing countries to address the digital divide. There may be a role for an international agency (such as ECOSOC or one of the other agencies within the United Nations) to oversee these developments. The taxes collected by each country would need to be remitted to the supervising agency, and decisions made on the distribution of these funds. This would require the establishment of governance and accountability structures.

The intangible nature of the knowledge economy, and the difficulty in controlling cross-border transactions and communications, raises issues as to what revenue-generating activities (ICT or otherwise), or organisations, could be the subject of the tax. If spectrum is viewed as a global good, then there may be an opportunity to raise funds by imposing a levy or tax on a percentage of the money raised through spectrum auctions. Obviously, any taxation proposal requires a significant administrative infrastructure for collection and enforcement.

However, the real barrier is not the technicalities of a "digital tax", but the development of international political consensus. This would require a lobbying campaign to develop awareness of the deepening crisis in global knowledge creation; as stated previously, research priorities are determined by the financial returns, rather than by global need and human welfare and security. There is a role for UNESCO and other concerned agencies, governments, NGOs and interest groups, to advocate the need for a sustainable funding mechanism for universal access to information which is a global public good.

Role of Information Institutions

What are the distinctions and interplay between electronic and traditionally published public domain information? What is the role of traditional information institutions in respect of the development of virtual (digital) libraries and archives?

Libraries are part of the social strategy in democratic societies and have a mission to promote learning and knowledge creation, to support the information needs of their user communities, and to provide the means for an informed citizenry. These "public good" objectives are in conflict with the philosophies of economic rationalism which underlie the debate on the global knowledge economy.

This trend has serious implications for the conservation and growth of the information commons, "historical democratic premises for providing open access to information through libraries are being challenged as information resources become a form of capital and as more aspects of information infrastructure are privatised." Libraries and archives are a key source of public domain information, yet they are coming under increasing pressure in the digital era.

There are competing predictions about the future of virtual or digital libraries and electronic publishing. The first scenario is one of radical transformation, where print-on-paper is replaced by electronic publication as the norm. Electronic access will result in an unprecedented breadth and multiplicity of information sources. There will be fundamental changes in the relationship between authors and publishers, information institutions and their constituencies; in particular, far less dependency on intermediation and on conventional channels of access and distribution. Information institutions (such as traditional libraries, archives and museums) and publishers, which rely on physical collections or print-on-paper, will have to transform themselves or face extinction.

The other view of the future is that, "we are in the process of evolutionary, not revolutionary, social change toward an information-oriented society. This thesis sees digital technologies as an extension or continuation of earlier technology (for example, computer networks are a continuation of earlier communication technologies such as the telegraph, telephone, radio and television)." The technology develops in response to people's social choices. Those institutions which had to manage these technologies will adapt their practices to the new generation of technology, "Electronic publishing will become ever more important, but only for certain materials that serve certain purposes. Print publishing will co-exist with other forms of distribution. Although relationships between institutions will evolve, publishers, libraries and universities serve gate-keeping functions that will continue to be essential in the future. More activities will be conducted online, with the result that face-to-face relationships will become ever more valued and precious."

Both scenarios (described respectively as the discontinuity and continuity theory) are an exaggeration. The third prediction which seems more plausible has been described as the, "co-evolution of information technology, human behaviour, and organisations". None of these exist in isolation; they influence the development or responses of the other, so that, "technology pushes, while demand pulls".

The co-evolution theory is supported by current trends in the print and electronic publishing markets. Demand continues unabated for print (on paper) material and the number of bookshops continues to grow. Various delivery mechanisms and media co-exist rather than replace or extinguish the older more traditional means of communication (whether this is oral tradition relying on human memory, hand worked manuscripts and other works, typesetting and print, radio or TV). If anything, the advent of digital information and electronic access promotes interest in information generally so both electronic and print media benefit.

Each has their own niche. There is also duplication with the availability of some information in both printed and online media. While electronic publishing will transform some information markets (especially due to the shifting economics of scholarly publishing and to the increasing array of formats), and while it will continue to occupy an important niche, it is unlikely that it will ever extinguish print. Similarly, the value-added services of editing, marketing and distribution should result in a continuing role for publishers.

The information overload of the information age will ensure there is also a place for librarians. However, their role will no longer be as gatekeeper but as interpreter. The advances in navigation tools may facilitate retrieval, but by opening up vast reservoirs of knowledge previously inaccessible, it has also ensured that there should be a role for those who have the skills to know how to maximise search potential and how to interpret the results of the search process.

This is because, "access to information does not of itself signify competitive advantage or guarantee the user becoming more informedÿÿ Tapping the unique items of useful information and (through synthesis and analysis) seeing the pattern in them—this is the art of online search today".

The development of digital technologies, particularly online services and electronic publishing, and their impact on conventional channels of distribution and access, are perceived as a threat by many scholars, librarians, print publishers and distributors. In particular, the move from print (on paper) to electronic publishing is seen as a major challenge.

The acquisition of research information (in the form of journals and scholarly collections) by universities and reference libraries is declining; this is despite an increase in the output of the world's research information. Meanwhile, there is a trend to cut the budgets of research libraries, yet the costs of maintaining their information infrastructure, particularly for science and technology journals, is escalating.

Librarians are under serious pressure as they struggle to maintain both print and electronic resources. In the case of journals, these often relate to the same body of information. The cumulative effect of these trends has been described as a "crisis" in scholarly communications.

The irony is that electronic publishing is well suited to scholarly works because, for example, research journals have a relatively small audience and therefore suffer from the lack of economies of scale (making the cost of these collections prohibitive). Electronic access becomes critical in a research environment where the number and price of scholarly journals are growing at a greater rate than these libraries can afford. The result is that libraries can only acquire an ever decreasing proportion of the scholarly literature which should be available to their user community.

This perceived crisis has prompted collaborative efforts among research organisations, and numerous initiatives among industrialised countries, which advocate a strategic rethink of their national research information infrastructure.

There has been much speculation about the impact of digital information, including the shift to electronic publishing, on the information market; particularly, its implications for different pricing models. Some of these impacts which are relevant to electronic publishing have been summarised as follows, "Some proprietary positions in simple distribution chains are likely to erode as a result of disintermediation and intense competition. Reduced production costs and pressure to avoid residual transaction costs may force vendors away from complex pricing models.

For example, usage-based pricing may give way to subscription pricing. Such dynamics will lead to new business models and, in small markets where users are also producers, may lead to new institutional arrangements for managing life-cycle costs of information. Similarly, as production decrease, the cost of information may be assimilated by the underlying infrastructure or assumed by advertisers and other interests.

This trend may be seen in the pricing of online services and in the massive volunteering of content on the World Wide Web. This applies to editorial and navigation functions traditionally performed by publishers and libraries to be performed increasingly by individual authors and users."

Print (on paper) publishers face very high fixed first copy costs. Competition creates pressures to price at marginal cost, but most publishers face similar cost structures. The significance of electronic publishing is that it introduces a medium with the potential to reduce significantly first copy costs.

While the above quote focuses on the changes brought about by digital media and electronic publishing, particularly on pricing models, in other respects there is much that remains unchanged. For example, publishing adds value to authoring.

The publisher provides services in the form of copy editing, proofing, typesetting, printing and binding. It may also be responsible for marketing and distribution. While some of these services are rendered obsolete by electronic access and electronic publishing, others remain relevant. For example, electronic journals will still require distribution skill in the form of server administration, backup maintenance and network management.

The conclusion, in economic terms, is that, "Publishing adds significant value to authoring. The digital revolution is changing sources and amounts of value added, but not eliminating it.

The costs of some functions are decreasing rapidly, but other costs are not. Meanwhile, as new information services are developed, new opportunities for publishing value-added are also created." This comment recognises that one of the most significant consequences of electronic publishing is the opportunity created by unlimited new formats and functionality. These include the ability to search, sort, display and to use hyperlinks between documents and from citations to original sources.

Accordingly, another consequence of electronic publishing and electronic access are the opportunities to find new value from different uses of content and to recover the cost of these services through differential charges. The presumptions which make this possible are that different users value different uses or content differently; electronic access makes it possible to retrieve various aspects of information and in different forms.

The economics of this result has been described as follows, "Electronic access enables both publishers and libraries to engage in new product bundling and non-linear pricing schemes. The first will often involve unbundling of traditional journal components, and then rebundling in a greater variety of packages, some of them customised for customers, or customisable by them. Non-linear pricing is facilitated by lower transaction cots for fine-grained purchases, and feasible direct usage monitoring by the publisher or library.

New bundling and pricing schemes are enabling technologies: they liberate previously unrealised sources of value from existing content and from new value-added services. For example, bundling can do a better job of extracting revenue from users who value the same content differently. Non-linear pricing can "sort" users by their preference for new services, and extract more of their differing values. Publishers earn returns on their innovations that can offset fixed publishing costs, and by spreading those fixed costs over more streams of revenue, can recover them with less quantity distortion and vulnerability to competition. In a competitive publishing environment, consumers get to keep most or all of the newly liberated surplus (excess of value over cost)."

Any consideration of the interplay between print and electronic publishing, such as cost comparisons, must recognise that electronic access changes the profile of available services and their quality.

Libraries are much more than information collections and inventories. They are also social institutions which support and serve the information needs of their user communities in a variety of ways, "A library is more than books and bricks. If it is successful, it supports a sense of community among its users, as an archive of its collective knowledge and as a resource for its future. Yet digital libraries thus far have tended to be digitised versions of card catalogs, books' and journals, and as such do not evoke a sense of community."

One of the most successful features of the Internet has been the use of its networking capabilities (the World Wide Web, e-mail, bulletin boards and chat rooms) to develop virtual user communities. Many libraries currently take advantage of this facility to extend their library community into the networked or virtual world.

We can expect the next phase of development for digital libraries to make the link between facilitating access to digital collections which are of relevance to a particular constituency and the networking ability provided by the Internet. Another observation concerning the importance of personal human interaction is that the strongest sense of virtual community develops when network communications are reinforced with face-to-face meetings. Therefore, it is reasonable to assume that physical libraries, or libraries as institutions, will never disappear, but will evolve so that digital libraries become an extension, rather than a replacement, of the current information infrastructure.

An important distinction between print media and electronic publishing has its origin in the tangible nature of print-on-paper. A book is a physical item, a product. There is a tendency to treat digital information as a service. This could have long lasting effects on access to information. By paying for a book, the purchaser owns it forever. By paying for the right to access information online, such as under a licence or a subscription service, there is no guarantee that the user (purchaser) will retain access to the previously available information, "Complex and difficult balances will need to be established, as information increasingly becomes an event to be viewed or experienced, rather than packaged as an artefact to be kept and archived."

The other consequences of the widespread trend towards user pays licensing models have already been referred to in paragraph, in respect of the undermining of the fair use doctrine. There are strong reasons as to why knowledge creators and the holders of intellectual property rights need to retain a degree of control in many (but not all) circumstances.

However, "There also needs to be a place for the capture of cultural history and social memory - at some point events are both common enough (widely enough available to the public) and important enough to become part of that record. Social agreements need to be developed about the status of information as event, and these agreements need to be reflected in the law and in practice; the legitimate interests of artists, commerce, and society must all be balanced."

The circumstances in which information can be considered a "publication" has significant consequences for public access to information. Public access to facts and ideas in published works is regarded in many jurisdictions as part of the copyright normative structure. When information is published in a public way, there are public access expectations. There is therefore a body of law, fundamental to the current intellectual property rights regime, which relies on the distinction between information which is published or unpublished, which is public or private.

For print (on paper) information, the distinction between what is published, as opposed to unpublished, has historically been reasonably clear. In the digital environment, these distinctions have become blurred, creating concerns about the IPR status of certain information. Examples include the situation where information is posted to a closed user site, requiring password access, or else via an intranet. Another difficult situation is where the control systems of the computer allows multiple layers of conditional access.

The use of hyperlinks has prompted debate over the rights to access and link other sites. The dynamic nature of postings is another issue, where it can be unclear as to whether or not a work is still evolving or is a completed draft. As a result of these features of the technology, it has becoming increasingly difficult to determine what information is unconditionally available as public domain information, "What appears to be a relatively simple distinction in the print world—published vs private - becomes complex in the digital world The concern also exists that more informational works will be distributed in ways that will be labelled as private, keeping them inaccessible to the public and out of our cultural and intellectual heritage."

The problems associated with the preservation of digitised archives pose a major challenge to the fate of historical and cultural records in the digital era. Under the doctrines of first-sale and fair use, and the copyright deposit schemes, libraries have been able to purchase a book or journal for inter-library lending and can take steps to preserve it indefinitely so that it can continue to be made available to the public.

With electronic publishing, a vast amount of digital information is never formally published, with the result that these works are not caught by the legal requirement to ensure that a number of copies are deposited in the national public library. As discussed previously, there is an unresolved problem of the line between publication and limited distribution becoming quite blurred or ambiguous. It is no longer sufficient to rely on deposit rules which are dependent on a criterion of "publication".

Another difficulty is that with a printed book, a legal (copyright) deposit scheme is manageable in that it requires a finite number of copies to be deposited in the relevant library or archive. The problem is how to ensure the same certainty can be achieved with electronic access to digital information, as this cannot be open-ended access; and especially if access is more complex, due to the linking of texts, than just allowing access to a single document or journal format.

There are many technical barriers to preserving digital public domain information. The long term archiving of this information necessitates storage on media which have a long life span, can be easily retrieved and viewed, despite changes to the technology There is an additional dilemma of how to capture dynamic and interactive digital works, and at what point during their evolution or creation process.

As storage media deteriorate, it must be possible to allow the systemic copying, for conservation and preservation purposes, of digital material from older media to the current generation. This needs to be permissible under copyright laws. This issue is not just limited to the copyright of the digital information itself, but also to the intellectual property status of its medium.

If digital information can only be read through the use of proprietary software, then this medium must also be migrated from one generation of equipment to the next. Quite apart from the impact on the availability of information, the use of automated rights management systems (which can control subsequent reuse of that information), will complicate and impede the ability to preserve information which has been protected or is controlled in this way.

The strategies to combat obsolescence may require copyright changes to allow migration from one storage technology to another and to resolve the tension between reformatting and the creation of derivative works. The technical problems of managing digital information must be addressed because of their serious impact on the amount and availability of information which becomes part of the information commons, through libraries, archives and other information institutions.

The traditional physical notion of an information institution places more certain boundaries on its form and services. The ability of the global network to link digital resources will result in many different models and hybrid forms of information institutions and services. The role of the conventional library includes selecting, collating, organising, conserving and providing access to information on behalf of a community of users. The particular practices of the library have evolved through the centuries, adapting to changes in information media. The libraries of the future will follow the same evolutionary pattern in modifying their design and capabilities to respond to the latest generation of digital media and electronic access.

The future design of the digital library will be of critical importance to its role of conservator, promoter of and conduit to public domain information. The debate over the future design of digital libraries has moved beyond the early emphasis on data bases and information retrieval, to view them, "as an extension, enhancement, and integration of information retrieval systems and of multiple information institutions."

Despite the emphasis of such definitions on the full lifecycle of creating, seeking, using, preserving and disposing of information resources, the World Wide Web is still not seen as a "global digital library". There are a number of reasons for this view, including: the incompleteness of its content (with available digital content being only a tiny proportion of the total of printed materials available); its lack of coherence and cataloguing; its lack of standards of validation; the ineffectiveness of its tools for information retrieval; and, lack of a specific user community.

The key influence on the emergence of digital libraries is intellectual property policy. It will shape the future design of the virtual or digital library. The reason is that it is the modes of access and use of the information by users that creates the value in respect of information, and this is controlled by intellectual property policy.

There are parallel systems of intellectual property, resulting in the parallel emergence of digital libraries. There are three very different kinds of digital libraries which have been described by Peter Lyman as follows: copyright, where collections have been placed online by research libraries and individual academics (by digitising their paper collections and placing them in the public domain on the World Wide Web); gift exchange, where authors volunteer their own intellectual property by placing it directly on the World Wide Web and into a type of global public domain; contract, where publishers create an electronic commerce library by charging online fees for service to access information protected by password and encryption technologies (and in that sense the information is on the private domain of the Internet).

Lyman also comments on the implications of this third model, contract-based access ("the e-commerce library"), for the future of public domain information. He notes that the primary unsolved problem is the social inequality implied in this model and draws a disturbing inference from any concept of "universal access" which is modelled on telecommunication concepts of universal service, "The use of contracts formalises the transition from an information policy-based on public libraries to a system of "universal access", modelled after American telecommunication policy. With universal access, public access to the network is subsidised, but the consumer must pay for the information used. Previously, the fai use exemption to copyright has subsidised information access for education purposes. Today, "universal access" is being defined as access to the Internet itself rather than to educational information on the Internet. Thus information flows in the digital library of the future will likely be governed on a per capita or fee for service basis; on the other hand, the argument goes, these revenues will fund the development of vast high quality online libraries."

Another factor in the design of the digital library of the future is the need to know the psychological, sociological, economic, political and cultural factors that motivate people to create, use, seek and acquire information. What are the users' criteria for selecting and evaluating digital information? Of particular importance are judgements about quality. For example, one of the key findings of the writings on the economics of scholarly information is that, despite the problems of high fixed costs and relatively low marginal costs, it is the perceived value of the scholarly journal which is the most important differentiator in determining price. Factors such as the prestige and quality of the journal and the requirement on academics to publish as a measure of their academic performance, are significant influences on price and demand.

Documents are created for a purpose and often within a community context, therefore its very important to understand the "social life" of a document or particular information. This is necessary in order to design digital libraries that support the behavioural context of their information collection.

In order for digital libraries to become more than a metaphor, and to evolve into a virtual information institution capable of conserving and providing access to public domain information, there is a need for strategies on a number of issues:

— How to manage the co-evolution process in collections where libraries are required to maintain both print and electronic versions, and collections are becoming more hybrid and distributed.

— How to ensure that information systems are useable and able to serve large and diverse communities; this will require initiatives ranging from rules and standards for metadata, new methods of auto-indexing, more sophisticated searching and navigational tools (other than based on word frequency or source type).

— The organisational requirements of the move from independent to linked systems, and from supporting isolated individual access to knowledge networking.

— The need to consider the social context and to make digital libraries and networks relevant to, and able to serve, multiple communities; in particular, how to achieve the balance between libraries tailored to a specific user community and the need for interoperability within the global information infrastructure.

— The need to enable users to bridge the numerous formats, representations and languages of individual digital libraries; this highlights the importance of standards for data exchange, portability, interoperability and for physical connections among devices.

— The importance of libraries and librarians remaining highly visible, despite being part of a well-functioning information structure, in order to emphasise their critical role in maintaining an information commons and facilitating universal access.

— How to scale up from the current level of ICT and the Internet to a truly "global digital library" that is much more complex with more diversity and greater numbers of users. In addition to the connectivity issues of more bandwidth and speed, "scaling requires new methods for seeking, creating, using, managing, preserving, and delivering information. It requires new economic models for allocating network resources. New policy models are needed for protecting and managing intellectual property, privacy and security, both domestically and internationally."

— Digitisation is still very expensive due to the labour costs of handling each page for scanning. The preservation of the electronic record is also an expensive process due to the deterioration of the media, obsolescence of the equipment and the need for software upgrades, and the need to maintain dynamic links to other systems.

— The above references to standards, bridging and interoperability include the many issues to be resolved in terms of future formats of metadata. This is information about what exists, in what form and where it can be located. As well as being descriptive, metadata may also have a functional purpose. It has a critical role to play in facilitating access to public domain information. There is a tension between the need for specialised formats serving specific user communities and the need for sufficiently generic formats to enable search and retrieval of information despite it being located in different discipline areas or across various domains.

The role of the librarian must change in response to electronic publishing and electronic access. Librarians are an example of value-add, however, with the by-passing inherent in online access, the concept of value-adding becomes blurred and there is the threat of disintermediation. Librarians could lose much of their gatekeeper role, due to the multiplicity and availability of databases and systems, and the increasing sophistication of search tools and retrieval processes.

However, there will be an increasing need for information intermediaries to make sense of the vast array of resources and information overload. The digital library will move beyond the collection of content on behalf of a user community and facilitating information retrieval, to the cycle of creating searching and using information, with the development of the services that are implicit in this role.

There will also be technical roles in the development of information infrastructure for standards, interoperability, document and reference linkage, and collating the digital sources for specific user communities. In the future, the role of librarians will evolve: "from collection builder to knowledge prospector,from classifiers, cataloguers, indexers to metadata developers and publishers. from information retrieval specialists to knowledge navigators and expedition guides. from reference librarians to information analysts and knowledge interpreters. librarians will need to become effective collaborators as well as teachers."

In terms of rethinking the role of librarians in the information age, the focus should not be on digital libraries but on universal access (to information). The relevant questions are, "What resources and services are needed, and by whom? Which are essential and which are desirable? What infrastructure is needed to support information resources and services? Who should provide them?" In the context of an Information Society for All and the debate over universal access, the "public domain" has evolved into a term of art. What we understand by this term is that the public domain is an intellectual commons which is the essential foundation for an informed and participatory society. It is critical for education, research and knowledge-creation. Therefore, the public domain has come to represent that body of information resources and knowledge where it is perceived that there are greater public benefits to be derived from sharing and disseminating that information to the broadest possible audience; the corollary is that any implied exclusivity (in terms of control over this process) is to be actively resisted. The concept of a public domain is readily transportable to the global environment and is captured by the phrase "global public good".

The hope and promise of the knowledge society is that it will ultimately enhance the quality of life for its citizens, reinforce social cohesion and result in economic opportunity and inclusion. The caution is that the profound changes brought about by the communications technologies of the information age, are resulting in increased inequities. The erosion of that body of knowledge and cultural and social heritage, which is captured in the information commons, takes us down the path of a deepening digital divide.

We are also at a critical stage in the formulation of the policies, regulatory frameworks, and infrastructure, that will comprise the future global knowledge society. This is despite a lack of understanding about the dynamics of the information economy and the social and global impacts of the emerging information and communications technologies. For these reasons, there is an urgent need to advocate the special role that public domain information must play in the future fabric of the knowledge society.

It is therefore essential to promote a concept of "public domain information" and to ensure its recognition in information policy, law and ICT design. This means resisting measures which create a "pay-per-view digital library", thereby resulting in the "enclosure of the information commons".

Access to information ought to be a fundamental value. The decision as to what information should be publicly available, and on what terms, is a very complex issue; in particular, the economics of knowledge-creation and the competing rights of the numerous information stakeholders. Even so, there are emerging expectations as to what types of knowledge and information are of such significance for human advancement as to merit their "protection" from appropriation; the public interest in ensuring its availability must prevail over the private interests in that information.

As the Human Development Report notes, "knowledge is the new asset and globalisation's rules have set off a race to lay claim to knowledge". It points out that the past decade has proven the tremendous potential of global communications to provide information, enable empowerment and raise productivity, but it has also exposed the risks of polarising societies and threatening greater marginalisation of those left out and left behind. What lies in between is proactive policy. The conservation of the information commons is one such policy, the implementation of which now requires the development of specific strategies and actions.

6

Responsibilities of Information Systems

In dealing with information systems, public sector organisations have to cover eight main areas of responsibility: information systems planning, organisational structures and staffing, data management, computing and data management architecture, information systems development, information technology acquisition, training, and technical support. Adopting a centralised approach to these responsibilities can bring efficiency benefits, but requires some severe constraints to be overcome. Adopting a decentralised approach can help spread computing in the organisation, but is often wasteful.

Public Sector Information Systems

A range of potential information systems (IS) responsibilities arises in the public sector, from which eight can be identified:

— *Information systems planning*: the priorities set for new information systems, for the applications of new information technology (IT), and for other IS-related changes.

— *Organisational structures and staffing*: the organisational structures used to support the information systems function, and the staffing of that IS function.

— *Data management*: the way in which data is structured and controlled in the organisation.

— *Computing and data management architecture*: the way in which IT is spread and connected throughout the organisation, and the way in which data structures and processing are divided across the IT.

— *Information systems development*: the who and how by which new information systems are analysed, designed, constructed and implemented.

— *IT acquisition*: what information technology is procured and how it is procured.

— *Training*: what skills are required in training, how that training is to be delivered, and to whom.

— *Technical support*: the way in which IT is installed, maintained, repaired and otherwise supported in its operation.

There are three possible approaches to these IS responsibilities which will be discussed in this chapter:

— *Centralised*: decisions are taken at the most senior or central level.

— *Decentralised*: decisions are taken at some level lower than the most senior; typically by individual work units within the organisation or even by individual staff.

— *Core-periphery*: decisions are taken at *both* senior and lower levels, either separately or in an integrated manner.

Centralised Approach

Many public sector organisations began their 'computing careers' by adopting a centralised approach, and there are continuing drives to maintain centralisation. These drives include particularly the desire of senior public managers to control the costs, pervasive impacts, and potential failures associated with information systems. Managers are also driven by the desire to achieve the potential benefits of centralised approach, including those listed below.

A well-planned centralised system holds data used across the organisation in one place, allowing all staff to access it. This makes it both faster and easier to undertake organisation-wide activities. Central planning and operation also allows compatible technology and skills to be introduced. Exchange of hardware, software and staff between organisational systems and units therefore becomes much easier.

One main intention of centralised approaches is to have a single version of any particular information system for the whole organisation, and to store any item of data once and only once. As a result, there is no wasted effort, no wasted storage capacity, and no inconsistency of data. A centralised approach to information systems provides an organisational focus for learning and for control. This is likely to produce higher quality information systems and can also reduce costs by:

— avoiding the decentralisation problems of non-functioning or malfunctioning systems,

— avoiding the decentralisation problems of inadequate security, maintenance and documentation, and by

— allowing technology purchases and system developments that are not organisational priorities to be blocked.

Achievement of scale economies

Centralised approaches allow most activities to be undertaken more cheaply per unit. Items purchased externally – computers, software packages, consumables, staff training, etc. – can be decided upon once and then bought in greater bulk. Activities undertaken internally – from system development to implementation and maintenance, and management of all these processes – cover a greater number of staff.

However, centralised approaches are beset by problems, some of which are outlined in this and the following section. First, there are constraints: most public sector organisations encounter considerable barriers if they attempt to develop a centralised approach to information systems, as described below.

Technical constraints

Where decentralised information systems, manual or computerised, are already in place, technical barriers to centralisation may be immense. Indeed, computerisation may create 'electronic concrete' that increases these barriers. The barriers include differences between existing decentralised IS in everything from data definitions to software to computing and network systems. Technical barriers also include the need to create some form of interconnection – typically a computer network – between the different organisational units whose systems are to be centrally controlled.

Resource constraints

Centralised approaches require the commitment of four key resources: money, time, people, and skills. For many public organisations, a centralised approach may not be possible because of financial constraints; because staff are too busy on other things; or because no-one has the confidence or capabilities to undertake the necessary planning and co-ordination tasks.

Perceptual constraints

The perception of information itself is a constraint to centralised approaches. Information is intangible, and public managers rely heavily on informal information in their decision making. Information is therefore perceived in a way that makes it hard for senior public managers to appreciate some of the key tenets of a centralised approach: that information is an organisation-wide resource; that it has a cost; that it can provide value for the public sector; that it needs to be managed; and so on.

Partly related to this is the perception of costs and benefits. The costs of decentralised approaches – of wasted efforts, of organisational inflexibility, of user time diverted from other activities – are frequently hidden. The benefits, such as managers being able to do what they like, are fairly obvious. For centralised approaches, by contrast, the equation is often the other way round. The resources required for the implementation of centralised approaches require an overt, 'up-front' commitment. The benefits, though, may be rather intangible, and it can be difficult to shift the perceived cost-benefit balance in favour of centralisation.

Political constraints

Information is a component of power. Any attempt to alter the pattern of information flows – which adoption of a centralised approach invariably involves – means a possible loss of power that will be resisted.

This is a particular problem for the public sector given the political antagonisms caused by the need to fight over limited resources. Resistance manifests itself most often in an unwillingness to share data with other individuals or groups. Differing political agendas that create barriers to data sharing also exist. People find it hard to think of "my data" or "our data" becoming "the organisation's data".

Political barriers to the centralised allocation of other information system resources such as money, equipment and staff, can also arise.

Cultural constraints

Barriers and antagonisms between decentralised units can undermine any hope of drawing them together for a centralised approach to information systems. At times, these barriers seem to derive from a 'them and us' attitude that is akin to modern-day tribalism. These cultural barriers are seen in the different mindsets that create quite different views of the world between groups; in the different jargon they use in communication; and in the different issues and people they value. This makes it hard to centralise.

Lack of trust deriving from such barriers is seen to prevent the type of co-operation required for centralised approaches to information systems. It is, indeed, the IT business which has helped to spread *NIH*: the *not invented here* mentality that rejects information systems for the simple reason that someone else developed them.

Structural constraints

Structural barriers to centralised approaches in the public sector are found both within and between public sector organisations:

— *Top managers*: do not understand IT or its possible uses in their organisation. They will resist centralised approaches they fear they cannot understand or control.

— *IT staff*: do not understand the public organisation's business and are only really interested in the technology. This prevents centralised approaches being business-led, and leaves them being technology-led. Such approaches, if developed at all, therefore address only IT, not data or information systems or business objectives.

— *Mainstream staff* can be divided into:

— *Computer illiterates* who feel threatened by IT, its jargon and its association with change and the unknown; they will resist centralised approaches because of their fears, and

— *Computer literates* who want to pursue their own agenda without seeing the need for co-ordination of IT activities or for 'interference' from IT staff; they will undermine centralised approaches by trying to develop their own information systems.

In addition, there may be members of the most difficult staff group – *semi-literates* – who think they know all about IT, are vocal in expressing their opinions, but who in practice understand little about the technology and nothing about information systems.

The gaps are partly those of objectives, of knowledge, and of culture, with each group talking a different 'language', holding different worldviews and/or interests, and not trusting the others. However, gaps also relate to the public organisation's structures for information systems responsibility. For example, a centralised IS unit may remain independent with little involvement from mainstream managers unless it is explicitly staffed and structured to create that involvement.

These structural problems – especially when combined with political and cultural barriers – seem likely to increase during reform processes of decentralisation, privatisation and outsourcing that lead to fragmentation of public sector organisations. We are then faced with the paradox that public sector reform simultaneously increases the requirement for, but decreases the possibility of, centralised approaches to IS.

Some of these barriers also exist to decentralised approaches, and we should recognise them as *barriers to change in general* rather than to one or other approach. However, the barriers to centralised approaches appear greater and, the more strategic and centralised the approach, the greater these barriers are likely to be.

Disadvantages of centralised approaches

Even if the listed constraints were to be overcome, centralised approaches can produce some disadvantageous outcomes. One obvious disadvantage of a centralised approach – as already noted above – is the high level of overt resource costs. Other disadvantages are described below.

Heavy time consumption

Centralised decisions and actions are more time-consuming than a decentralised approach because of: the additional time it takes for information to flow up the organisation as an input to centralised decisions; the additional time it takes to collate information from a variety of different decentralised locations as an input to centralised decisions; and the additional time it takes for implementation information to flow down the organisation. The result can be inordinate delays in the process of information systems development.

Limited ability to meet user needs

Centralised approaches necessarily mean that priority goes to those systems which are seen as important by some select and centralised staff group. The priorities of the periphery – both individuals and individual work units – may not be addressed. Consequences of this failure to meet user requirements may include:

— a backlog of user applications awaiting development,

— limited use or even total failure of centrally-planned information systems, and

— poor quality of data within these systems, since users will not be motivated to maintain data quality.

The frequent outcome is that end users subvert central controls and impose a *de facto* decentralisation.

The greater the amount of central planning that has gone into an information systems decision, and the longer that decision is therefore intended to provide guidance for the organisation, the less flexibility it offers the organisation to cope with internal or external changes. The British Army fell into this trap when it produced its first IT strategy. The strategy document ran to 800 pages and created a 'strait-jacket of detail' that meant managers 'felt like prisoners of over-rigid procurement methodologies and ... over-rigid IT strategies and management structures.'

Increased dependence and vulnerability

In general, centralised approaches to information systems make public sector organisations more dependent and more vulnerable for a number of reasons:

— greater numbers of staff rely on single information systems,

— greater reliance on a few key staff who plan, develop

and run those systems,

— greater technical complexity that makes problems harder to diagnose, and

— greater potential impact of data security breaches.

As a consequence management controls have to be far more rigorous (hence costly) with centralised systems.

It would seem that centralised approaches to public information systems are highly problematic. What, then, of decentralised approaches? As technology has become smaller, cheaper, easier-to-use, more reliable, and more powerful, so decentralised approaches seem to be an increasing possibility. Decentralisation may also be driven by a desire to remove control from central IT units, or by its perceived advantages, which include those listed below.

The closer the proximity of user and developer, the less the communication gap and the more likely it is that the developed system meets the users' real needs. At the extreme, where users are able to develop their own information systems, these are far more likely to meet their requirements than those developed by someone else.

Higher usage of computerised systems

This flexibility to fit local needs helps to explain the dramatic growth in computer use associated with decentralised approaches, such as end-user computing. Users are better motivated by such approaches and are far keener to take up computing when it directly supports their own interests and work.

Faster system development

The less the organisational distance between system user and system developer, the faster development of that system is likely to be. Again taking the extreme of end-user development, there will be no delay for the development of mutual understanding and no clash with higher priority information systems developments. This can help to overcome the staffing constraints and systems development backlog that often afflict centralised IS units. Other aspects of system use such as implementation, operation, troubleshooting and maintenance are also likely to occur more quickly under a decentralised regime.

Perceived lower costs

The 1990s have been characterised by a growing realisation that the costs of decentralised approaches are greater than anticipated because of many initially-unrecognised indirect costs. Nevertheless, some still argue that decentralised approaches present lower costs than centralised approaches. This is thanks to faster development, less miscommunication, greater fit to local needs, the greater emphasis on smaller computers, the greater emphasis on buying software packages rather than developing software in-house, and so on.

Decentralised approaches

However, just like their centralised counterparts, decentralised approaches are also beset by problems, some of which are outlined below and in the following section.

Many of the constraints to centralised approaches described above are, in fact, constraints to change in general. They are therefore also constraints to a decentralised approach and will not be reiterated in detail. Examples include:

— *Technical constraints,* such as heavy existing investments in a centralised system.

— *Resource constraints,* such as a lack of skills to support decentralised decision making and action on information systems.

— *Political constraints,* such as the unwillingness of those at the centre to change information flows, resource flows and associated organisational power.

However, it is rare for these constraints to be completely insurmountable, partly because of the great motivation of staff and individual work units to take some control over IT. At least some elements of IS decentralisation are therefore found in almost all public sector organisations.

Disadvantages of decentralised approaches

Even if the listed constraints are overcome, decentralised approaches can produce some disadvantageous outcomes.

Decentralised approaches can create information systems in different work units that are mutually incompatible. The resulting 'electronic concrete', like its centralised counterpart, constrains the scope of activities that organisations can undertake, or imposes substantial additional time and financial costs on those activities. In particular, strategic, organisation-wide activities are constrained. This can lead to anything from a difficulty in aggregating basic financial information across the organisation, to an inability to implement any strategic plans.

Barriers to sharing other resources, including human resources

There may also be an inability to share resources other than data if work units are allowed to set up their own separate systems. It may be hard to exchange hardware and software. Perhaps more importantly, each individual information system requires a unique set of skills for system development, implementation and operation. This makes it much more difficult for staff to move between different systems.

Duplication of effort

Apart from constraining what public organisations can do, decentralised approaches also tend to be very costly because units will often duplicate what others are doing. Duplication may cover:

— analysis, design and implementation of information systems,

— gathering and administration of data, and

— system operation, support and maintenance.

In addition, computer input, output, storage and processing capacity will all have to be duplicated. The unnecessary duplication of data (known as *data redundancy*) tends to be particularly problematic, yet it is quite common. For example, public organisations often store basic details of their employees many times over:

— on paper and on computer, and

— for personnel, for payroll, for training, and for other records.

This imposes additional costs in gathering, maintaining and updating data. In addition, because data about similar entities is held simultaneously in two or more different locations, it tends to become inconsistent. No-one then knows which, if any, version of the data is the most accurate or up-to-date. Trying to put together a reliable record involves a lot of chasing around and cross-checking.

Lack of learning and control

In addition to the extra direct costs that duplication imposes, there is an indirect cost of lost learning opportunities and limited cross-fertilisation of ideas. Decentralised approaches also necessarily mean limited central ability to plan and control, leading to a tendency for some decentralised systems to be developed and used without due care. The result may be a system that never works or does not work properly, with compromised data quality or system security.

Failure to achieve scale economies

As already noted, there are scale economies in information systems covering data, people, hardware and other resources. Decentralised approaches make all activities more costly, from buying computers to gathering data to training staff to system operation and maintenance. All of these problems can be largely summarised as: higher-than-desirable costs or a lower-than-desirable scope of public sector activities. The intangibility of many of the problems means that costs are not always recognised. For example, only in recent years have the true costs of end-user microcomputer ownership begun to emerge, with estimates up to US$10,000 or more per computer per year. Much of this is the cost of staff time taken up when users provide support to other users and when PCs are used for non-job-related or other unproductive activities. Training, maintenance and administration costs also contribute.

Both the centralised and the decentralised approach can provide benefits for public organisations. Yet, at the same time, such approaches can be hard or impossible to implement, and can produce serious disadvantages for the organisation.

What is the way out of this quandary? One way forward is the adoption of a core-periphery approach that attempts to reconcile the push of the centralised approach with the pull of the decentralised approach. It does this in two ways.

First, through *integration*: drawing the centralised and decentralised approaches together into some kind of unified or compromise approach. Second, and more commonly, through *division*. This accepts that both centralised and decentralised approaches will be found, and then attempts to set some demarcation lines that will keep the two separate, thereby allowing them both to be accommodated.

A decentralised approach may be most economic for public organisations, because it saves on overt input costs. A centralised approach may be most efficient, because it avoids waste and duplication. But a successful core-periphery approach may be most effective because it can simultaneously provide:

— the control necessary to share key resources (including data), to avoid duplication, and to achieve economies of scale; and

— the freedom necessary to meet user needs, and to overcome blocks to IT usage and IS development.

Core-Periphery Approach

A core-periphery approach to IS planning involves strong and active participation of users and local units in the formulation of strategy.

The planning process may then involve decisions about other elements of the core-periphery approach: planning which data items are generic and which are specific; dividing out responsibilities for information systems development; and so on.

In line with other core-periphery elements, such plans may also aim to guide more than dictate. The successor to the UK Army's 800-page strategy document cited above, for example, was only 30 pages long. It provided a guiding framework, allowing for flexibility and local initiative.

Organisational structures and staffing

A core-periphery approach may involve a separation of central and local responsibilities, as described below for areas such as data management and IS development. However, another strand can be an attempt to close the 'ITernal triangle' gaps identified above. For example, there is likely to be some central IS unit with a co-ordination role in this approach. It may have a management structure that involves end users and senior staff as well as IT staff. It may also be underpinned by a relatively open philosophy that looks outside the unit and regards the end users as its customers. This, for example, has been the philosophy adopted in restructuring IT structures across the South African public sector.

One common application of the customer-oriented philosophy is to create an 'end-user support centre'. This is essentially an internal extension/outreach unit. It reaches out from the centre to support users on the periphery and to help them make best use of their information systems and technology.

Another example of core-periphery approaches is the attempt to hire or create *hybrid staff*. They understand both the context and work of a public sector organisation *and* the role, management and jargon of information systems.

Data management

A core-periphery approach to data management typically involves a division of responsibilities, such as that which has been adopted across the Canadian government.

This division defines the centre's role as being the management of 'generic' data items (i.e. those used across all or most of the organisation). Typical generic data items would include those about organisational employees, finances, projects and services.

The periphery's role would be to:

- make use of generic data,
- alter generic data only within certain centrally-determined controls, and
- control 'specific' data items (i.e. those used only by individuals or small groups), for example, those within a database of personal contacts.

Computing and data management architecture

The most common core-periphery computing architecture is the client/server model, in which computing power is divided between the central servers and the local client workstations. This architecture has now been adopted by vast numbers of public sector organisations worldwide.

For organisations moving straight from a manual or stand-alone system to a client/server model, the main decisions to be made concern how power and resources are to be divided between the server core and the client periphery. Organisations moving from a centralised to a client/server architecture have an additional decision to make: what to do with the centralised system, which will often be mainframe-based.

There are three main choices:

- scrap the mainframe and move over fully to the client/server system,
- run two architectures in parallel, or
- make the mainframe part of the client/server architecture.

Information systems development

A core-periphery approach to systems development can involve a division of responsibilities, for example, defining certain types of information system as suitable for central development, and others as suitable for decentralised/end-user development. Decisions about how to classify project proposals for particular information systems can be made by a joint team of managers with technical staff input. This team will allocate central resources only to projects meeting agreed criteria.

Candidates for central development might be those systems where one or more of the following applies:

— the system is critical to the functioning of the organisation,

— the system is to be used by more than one department,

— data is drawn from several different sources, and/or

— there are particular technical issues such as a very large database or a need for a fast response time.

Such systems are seen as too important, too cross-cutting, and/or too skill-intensive to be appropriate for decentralised development.

Candidates for decentralised development might be those systems where one or more of the following applies:

— the system is relevant only to the individual user or department,

— data is drawn only from an existing centrally-managed database or from a proposed locally-managed database, and/or

— processing or reporting requirements are subject to frequent change.

Such systems are seen as too small and/or too specific to be appropriate for central development.

A slightly different perspective would aim to create a division of responsibilities within the development of each individual information system. Decentralised users might be responsible for systems analysis, training, documentation, and ongoing support. Centralised IT staff might be responsible for design, construction, implementation, operation and maintenance of the system.

In the development of a new management information system to support reform of materiel requirements planning, for instance, the US Air Force Logistics Command involved users throughout the IS development lifecycle. Users were made responsible for current system analysis, requirements specification, review and acceptance of detail design, preparation of test data, setting of acceptance criteria and user acceptance. They were also involved with the testing and data conversion processes. Coupled with formal project management procedures, this helped to ensure a good fit between user needs and system outcomes.

Alternatively, the central role may just be one of quality assurance: end users or work sections are responsible for developing an application, but quality is assured in some way by the central IS unit. This may involve central guidelines on anything from development methods to data structures, or central testing of programs or documentation. Finally, a core-periphery approach may also attempt to bridge internal divisions and have shared responsibilities for systems development. It might do this by creating structures that bring different groups together or through processes that allow these groups to communicate with each other. Such structures may involve participatory or prototyping techniques of systems development. The Royal Netherlands Air Force adopted this last method through the mechanism of a management game involving the simulation of the entire organisational information system for a planned air base. Not only did this create a shared vision for change among participants, it also facilitated discussion of key issues, and created a sense of unity between those involved. As a result, this has been recommended as a standard approach to public sector change.

IT acquisition

Standards for IT acquisition bring many immediate and obvious benefits to organisations. Unfortunately, they may be resented by users and can be circumvented relatively easily by users who have any local control over finances. This is a sensitive area because those who control the information technology tend to control the information held by that technology. As we know this, in turn, is a component of organisational power.

Core-periphery approach

A core-periphery approach to acquiring information technology therefore typically involves a mixture of 'carrot and stick': encouraging users to follow standards, and providing some limited sanctions for those who do not. It also typically involves a flexible approach to standards that allows users some local leeway within a set of boundaries.

The US General Services Administration and the UK's CCTA/Government Centre for Information Systems both make use of this approach, essentially providing public agencies with a shopping list of discounted items via central framework agreements. There is an 'opt in' model by which agencies can use these channels if they wish, but are not bound to do so.

Other elements of this approach may include:

— Reserving purchase of certain types of hardware (i.e. servers or all network hardware) for central decisions, or reserving purchases above some financial threshold for central approval, but allowing other purchases to be made by users. One intention here is to retain central control over the hardware that will form an organisation-wide technology infrastructure, such as telecommunications, but to relax other controls.

— Limiting the size of decentralised IT budgets. This avoids the extreme of a wholly centralised budget, which antagonises users and leads them to spend other budgets on IT. It also avoids the extreme of a wholly decentralised IT budget, which can lead to an unwillingness to fund any central services.

— Disseminating a set of minimum functional requirements (memory, disk size, chip, operating system capability, etc.) that all computers should meet, but allowing freedom of choice of model and supplier.

— Providing central advice, bulk purchase, installation assistance, training, and maintenance and repair services only for standardised hardware and software, but allowing users to diverge from this if they are willing to support themselves.

— Requiring that all networked IT conform to a certain specification, but allowing greater freedom for stand-alone information technology.

— Setting organisational standards for IT on a committee with strong user representation.

Other components of a core-periphery approach may include training and technical support.

Training

A common core-periphery approach is to centralise the planning of training for core information systems. Other training needs may be met, as requested, by end-user support centres or by informal training methods. There may also be central provision of access to open and flexible learning systems such as CD-ROM- or Internet/intranet-based training packages or videos.

Technical support

Given the very specialist nature of many repair and maintenance tasks, there are very high costs in leaving them to individual end users. Many organisations, therefore, have at least one IT support employee per department who takes on this role. Centralising this role even further can lead to response times and prioritisation that may seem poor from a user perspective. However, the more specialised the role, the more the arguments for centralisation.

In the case of both training and technical support (and other activities), consideration will have to be given to charges levied on work units or users for centrally-provided services. The benefit of charging (even a nominal sum) is that it induces users to take the services seriously. It will also transfer resources to the central IS unit. The problem of charging is that users may decide not to use the service, possibly creating additional costs for the organisation if equipment is then not used properly or wrongly repaired or left in an unusable condition.

7

Multilinguism in Cyberspace

The network-centered information society is just starting to evolve. Information and knowledge are forming one of the basic ingredients of such society. However, if that information and knowledge does not permeate the texture of the global society and be assimilated by the different societies worldwide, it will have a limited impact on the global community.

The convergence of computer and telecommunication technologies is changing the way we perform work, communicate with each other, do business transactions and make use of the different services. A profound impact on education, learning and acquiring knowledge does not need to be emphasized. Information presentation in visual images, sound and natural language either as text or speech is gradually becoming the norm. The Internet is creating a global platform where a worldwide forum is evolving that is becoming vital to economic, social and political success. However, all these developments create problems.

Examples of such problems are: access to much of the information may be available only to the computer literate and those who understand English. Also, due to the vast amount of information available, it is becoming hard to identify and select what is relevant that may satisfy a certain degree of credibility. The development of interfaces and components that help users to identify relevant information and then present it to them in the most appropriate manner according to the information content and their cultural and linguistic backgrounds is still lagging behind the rate of information growth. Language engineering is an endeavor in which language technologies are integrated and embedded into language-enabled services and products to support business in a global context and to facilitate interpersonal communication across languages.

The Role of Language Engineering Efforts now are concentrating in developing tools and standards that enable the creation of websites in several languages or in at least one non-Western language. Now an Internet standard (RFC 2070) based on Unicode supports HTML documents in practically every language. In particular, some of the features dealt with are: Markup of bi-directional text, i.e. test where left-to-right and right-to-left scripts are mixed and control of cursive joining behavior in contexts where the default behavior is not appropriate. Also, the HTTP which is the hypertext transfer protocol in use since 1990 is being internationalized.

The relevant aspects are character set labeling which ensures correct document interpretation and language negotiation which is used at a site to provide documents in the user?s language of preference.Language technology will help in designing and implementing the systems needed to effectively deal with information and knowledge in a number of ways. Speech recognition will help in interacting with a number of devices in our own native language. Also, information could be presented by generating speech. Understanding requests and browsing the vast amount of knowledge available is an essential component that can alleviate the problem of information overload and ensures that the relevant knowledge is accessed. It will also be possible to generate and present information in different languages through automated machine translation.

Language engineering will be essential for supporting global business in general and electronic commerce in particular. The success of any business will depend on the quality of information about its customers, its competitors and the market in general. The needed information has to be identified, extracted and presented in natural language either as text or speech. In general, language engineering will deliver the right information at the right time and in the language of the recipient.

Automated translation together with document management will improve the quality of service in a global marketplace. In general, success in globalization requires putting emphasis on localization. Some companies interested in international markets organize their effort in a number of activities that could be summarized as follows:

1. Developers organize a product so that linguistic components can be modified easily (internationalization).

2. Translators make the product available in different target languages.

3. Editors review each version to ensure that culture-specific items are not missed.

4. Marketing division takes care of localization to adapt the product to the local market.

The Internet is dominated now by the English language. However, due to the near future possibilities of widespread use, it is becoming essential to consider its multilingual nature.

Some efforts are being conducted in that respect ? e.g. the Babel project which is a joint initiative between Alis Technologies and the Internet Society. They are considering the world?s 20 main languages and are trying to study the actual distribution of languages on the Internet. Although the Internet penetration is not high at the moment in some regions, this is expected to change radically in the future. As an example, results of the Internet Domain Survey for Arab Countries is shown in Table 1 for January 1998.

Efforts now are concentrating in developing tools and standards that enable the creation of websites in several languages or in at least one non-Western language. Now an Internet standard (RFC 2070) based on Unicode supports HTML documents in practically every language. In particular, some of the features dealt with are: Markup of bi-directional text, i.e. test where left-to-right and right-to-left scripts are mixed and control of cursive joining behavior in contexts where the default behavior is not appropriate. Also, the HTTP which is the hypertext transfer protocol in use since 1990 is being internationalized.

Table 1 : Internet Domain Survey Arab Countries, January 1998

Domain	*Hosts*	*All Hosts*	*DuplicateNames*	*Level 2 Domain*	*Level 3 Domain*
ku	4057	4749	692	9	2925
eg	2013	16930	14917	7	191
ae	1940	1955	15	8	56
lb	1134	1377	243	7	59
om	670	671	1	16	20
ma	431	463	32	5	339
bh	338	339	1	2	4
jo	249	249	0	5	13
qa	189	191	2	5	9
tn	69	69	0	10	68
sa	37	37	0	4	6
dz	16	17	1	1	16
ye	10	10	0	7	6
ly	1	2	1	1	1
sy, sd, iq	0				
	11154	27059			

The relevant aspects are character set labeling which ensures correct document interpretation and language negotiation which is used at a site to provide documents in the user?s language of preference.

Multilingual Machine Translation Issues

There are many situations in which multilingual translation is needed. Translation from many languages into a single language will be required by large information gathering and processing organizations.

Translation from a single language into many languages will be required in the context of foreign trade when operation and other manuals for industrial equipment need to be translated into the language of the countries where the equipment is to be marketed.

Multilingual interlingual machine translation systems translate between a number of languages. In this approach, a universal language independent representation of text known as interlingua is developed. Therefore, the translation process is reduced to two phases: the analysis phase between the source language and the interlingua, and the generation phase from the interlingua to the target language.

For successful machine translation, detailed knowledge of the languages is required at many levels: lexicon syntax, semantics and discourse. It is very difficult to provide such linguistic knowledge for an entire language. However, if we consider only language in a particular domain much of this knowledge could be obtained.

The variety of language used in a given science or technology is not only much smaller than the whole language, but is also more clearly systematic in structure and meaning. Therefore linguists and computer scientists co-operate to study the properties of such specialized languages which are called sublanguages or controlled language. Each sublanguage has a distinctive grammar even though it is related to the grammar of the full standard language. Also, the theoretical problem of relating linguistic form to communicative function comes into sharper focus when individual sublanguages are examined.

Sometimes it is essential to distinguish between two translation activities. The first one is called localization (e.g. that used for computer manuals for end users) where it is important to adapt certain parts of the content and perhaps the style of presentation to a certain cultural and linguistic environment. The second one is called diffusion translation where the objective content must be strictly rendered in another language without addition and omission.

A brief outline will now be given for efforts related to Arabic/English translation. AppTek started an English-Arabic translator named TranSphere that uses Lexical Functional Grammar together with a general dictionary having 100,000 words. A number of domain-specific dictionaries have also been developed. This system could be either standalone or part of an integrated system.

Sakhr within Al-Alamiah Group [Sakhr, 1998] is also developing a translation scheme for Arabic-English and English-Arabic. It makes use of the available tools that have been developed before for morphological and syntactical analyzers, electronic dictionaries, semantic support together with a number of other development tools. It is also developing a general platform for dealing with Arabic computations.

IBM Egypt is also developing Machine Aided Human Translation schemes. ALIS, Inc. offers a solution that integrates core language-handling technology and translation products.

Electronics Research Institute in Egypt, in co-operation with the European Community is developing an English-Arabic and Arabic to English and German medical text translation. This is done in the framework of CAT2 (Computer Assisted Translation) which uses an interlingua approach. Also, some work related to ambiguity in Arabic language processing is being studied.

PRINCITRAN: In this system a large-scale lexicon is to be constructed for an interlingual machine translation system for Arabic, English, Korean and Spanish [Dorr, 1995]. For Arabic, the starting point was the use of the Alpnet bilingual Arabic-English online dictionary. Then automatic mappings between English glosses from Alpnet into LDOCE (Longman?s Dictionary of Contemporary English) codes were performed. The codes were then converted into thematic grids which were then exhaustively hand-verified.

Electronic Commerce and Multilinguality

Global market opportunities are now increasing rapidly and is going to use heavily the facilities introduced by the Internet. Thus, the advent of global electronic commerce will add an economic dimension to cultural and linguistic issues. In international trade, companies that adopt a multilingual, multicultural approach are expected to gain a competitive advantage over their monolingual, monocultural competitors.

Regarding business-consumer relations, the following language issues could be stated: The seller of goods or services must be able to publish information in the language and cultural convention of the customers (multilingual electronic publishing). The buyer of goods or services must be able to find, understand and compare information in his own language (multilingual information retrieval). Both buyer and seller must be able to interact naturally and effectively in a common language or across different languages.

There is a possibility that from the number of 5,000 to 6,000 languages spoken in the world today, only a few hundred will survive a century later. The pressure on languages can take different forms: economic, social, cultural, etc.. Usually, people directly affected are minorities, but their languages represent the linguistic diversity that has developed over the course of human history. Some linguists argue that language endangerment is serious with great humanistic and scientific consequences. Can new developments in the information age help in preserving some of these languages and thus save language diversity.

Information revolution is the global phenomenon that has an impact on all nations. Nobody can stay out of the Information Society. That is why nowadays problems of ethical, cultural and social type has an increasing value. Only in resolving these problems the Information Society can achieve the declared goal of globalization: to promote quality of life and sustain a cohesive development. Due to the advent of the Information Society UNESCO faces new problems demanding to define its role in new world communication processes. That is why the UNESCO strategy should embrace the wide range of activities:

- concentration on key structures of the Information Society;
- ethic problems of the Information Society and the Cyberspace;
- elaboration of information policy;

- the impact of the globalization processes;
- specific education ;
- forming networks;
- fulfilling projects for the Information Society

These problems demand thorough considerations and constant attention. Textual information remains the main form of demanded information for majority of interstate or global international networks such as INTERNET. Due to the rapid success of communication technologies active use of spoken and visual information is foreseen in the nearest future. Nowadays there are near 3000 spoken languages in the world and only 100 of them are written. Such a variety of languages under increased value of international contacts, high intensity of information flows of economic, political, scientific, technological and social types put forward as a priority task the development of human language technologies.

Multilingualism is an inevitable historical attribute of the international communication process. The notion "multilingual information society " solidly occupies the place in the range of problems discussed by computer science specialists and predefined strategic directions of many international organizations and companies dealing with information distribution and processing.

Human language technologies obtained the valid political understanding and support. At the third UNESCO Congress on Informatics and Education held in Moscow, July 1996, more than 40 countries representatives confirmed their willingness to participate in the establishing multilingual telematics support for educational needs.

The relevance of linguistic and cultural aspects of the Information Society in Europe has been stressed by the European Council meetings in Corfu, 24-25 June 1994, in Cannes, 26-27 June 1995 and on the G7 Conference of Ministers in Brussels, 25-26 February 1995. In May 1995 the European Commission has adopted the upcoming Fifth RTD Framework Programme which includes points devoted to developing human language technologies.

Technological Multilingualism

In the multilingualism problem there exists one important factor which usually slips out in discussions of this issue. The high level of technology of the modern civilization broadens the notion of multilingualism in information society including in it artificial intellectual electronic devices. This newly arisen complex communication structure forms the Cyberspace that is marked by extremely complex processes of control and self-development. In the Cyberspace the humanitarian multilingualism interacts with the technological multilingualism of communication protocols, computer interfaces, programming languages and data protection methods.

Communication multilingualism of computing devices is to some extent being solved by introducing conventional technological standards regulating data exchange and transformation processes. Different computers in networks can transmit information using standard popular protocols TCP/IP (Transmission Control Protocol / Internet Protocol), IPX/SPX (Internetwork Packet Exchange / Sequenced Packet Exchange) or SNA (System Network Architecture). Such protocols as FTP (File Transfer Protocol), HTTP (Hyper Text Transfer Protocol), address standard URL (Uniform Resource Locator), standard sluice interface CGI are in active use in the INTERNET.

High expressive possibilities of Web pages rely on implementations of HTML and Java languages. For protecting information from different forms of eavesdropping cryptographic protocols SET (Secure Electronic Transfer) , SSL (Secure Sockets Layer) and some others have been elaborated. The "hardware multilingualism" aggravates the problem of the humanitarian multilingualism in the Cyberspace.

It is interesting to note some resemblance in humanitarian and technical multilingualism. Communication multilingualism is stormy developing and to some extent repeats the dramatic way of human multilingualism. Here also numerous languages and dialects currently appear and die, conflicts of standards, programming languages and interfaces is an usual event. Any technological innovation can lead to the chain, or may be it will be better to say "domino", reaction of expressive and communication means. The Cyberspace evolution is marked by constant attempts to resolve problems of humanitarian and technological multilingualism. The general common base for advances in these areas are backed by developing theory of semiotic systems, artificial intelligence, translation methods, algorithmic analyses, evolution of discourse, technologies sustaining lingual engineering.

Multilingualism Challenge

Historically formed present situation presupposes two

general approaches for partial resolving the multinational communication problem. The first approach relies on the idea to adopt some universal unique well understanding language for invariant multilingual communication. The second approach lays on elaborating powerful technique for simulating expressive means of one language by expressive forms of another one.

There are known three main variants in implementation of the first mentioned above approach.

- For some definite restricted knowledge areas to use specialized formalized languages such as Latin for medicine, language of formulas for mathematics, etc. This approach can be applied successfully only to very restricted object areas and cannot embrace cultural or social aspect of communication.
- To create one general artificial universal language which is neutral to national peculiarities of language communication. The most known language of this class is Esperanto. The less known is Sanskrit. The main drawback of this approach as in the previous case above is its impossibility to fill the communication gap in expressing national cultural potential.
- To conveniently adopt the use of one of national language. There is one well-known very strong candidate to play this role. Domination in the world processes (trade, science, technology, culture, etc.) of English speaking countries led to the huge spread of the English as a communication language. There are 1 billion and 400 millions of English speaking people in the world. Only for 400 million of them this language is native. This means that for more than 1 billion of world population this language is the

second or even the third one. And we are all witnesses that domination of the English as the communication tool in the Cyberspace is spreading with more and more increasing feedback link. The positive aspect of this event is extending for other nations the rich world of English speaking countries in all its appearances. The negative aspect is that such a global language invasion contradicts to natural eagerness of other nations to preserve local cultural achievements and adequate lingual means of their presentation. Even in the field of technological documentation complete relying on not native language information can affect the reliability of elaborating systems. Moreover, due to its internal evolution and rapid changing the fixed international English language can never be framed.

The second approach, which is simulating expressive means of one language by expressive forms of the other one, is traditionally reduced to the translation process. Before the computer era a bilingual or a multilingual interpreter was a man. Under computer expansion the language translation problem has obtained a new content - an automated language translation. In its full context this problem relates to the very complex problems of formalizing natural language understanding and cognitive context which are very far from the final decision. Nevertheless there are some recent evident successes in this area. The number of commercial systems for machine translation, as well as other types such as spell-checkers, multilingual mailers, dictionaries, etc. is rapidly growing.

During the last two years a few multilingual services available within Internet appeared. Multilingual Communication Corporation (USA) is offering its powerful WEB.TRANS service for global business. The two main browsers providers for WWW, companies Alis and Globalink, include the multilingual support in their products. The Tango, multilingual browser, using the Alis technologies, is a high performance Web tool that allows users to display Web pages authored in any of over 90 languages, select the languages of its interface, automatically retrieve these pages in the language version user prefers and input a text in a wide variety of languages. Alice Technologies has brought together several leading companies in the language industry to create Columbus - a suite of communication and translation tools and services designed to offer corporations the most comprehensive, convenient and cost-effective solutions on the market.

There are other well-known companies offering a variety of multilingual solutions among them: ACCENT (Israel), Ajax Software Corp. (Russia), IBM, Intersol Brea, SYSTRAN (USA). We can also concentrate on activity of BIT Software, Inc. (Russia), as well as ABBYY Company, formerly BIT Ukraine. These software companies are famous by their multi-lingual products like Stylus Gigant (powerul heuristic translator from five European languages to Russian and visa versa), Lingvo (large hyper-text interactive dictionary), WebTranSite (online "transparent" Internet translator), etc.

There is one interesting frequently met feature of the multilingualism paradigm. Due to different historical reasons in one country (nation, popularity) there are two or several internal natural languages sharing the same information space. Such a situation exists in many NIS countries, Ireland, Canada, India, Benelux countries and in many others. Ukraine is the bilingual country where the Ukrainian language has the state status. In this case specific domestic features could complicate the international multilingualism problem. Furthermore, problems become really global, e.g., after 7 years of official independence, Ukraine doesn't even have fully defined symbol code page (380), because four or five existing standards are already widespread and it's difficult to change any of them right now. Sometimes (as in Ireland) politics can influence the multilingualism decisions.

Much attention is paid to the processes of creating computer supported information infrastructure in Ukraine. The State program of informatization in Ukraine has been approved by the government. This program is backed by some legislative basis. There are three juridical laws concerning the informatization program. The first law defines the concept of the informatization in Ukraine. The second one defines objectives of the program. And the third law determines the content of the program. We would like to stress that the our Center is the leading organization in forming the concept and the governmental program of informatization in Ukraine.

International Research and Training Center of Information Technologies and Systems

In the organization we present here intensive research and technological works in language engineering are carried out. Let us mention briefly some of them.

- Multilingual speech technology. The technology of natural speech recognition and synthesis in a few foreign languages is developing by the specialists of our center for more than twenty years. In 1986 -1991 in frames of UNESCO contracts the multilingual (7 languages) speech dialogue system RECH-121 for CDS-ISIS Micro has been created. The works in the direction to create oral vocabularies-translators, dictating machines, machines simulating a human voice, individual speech passports, systems of multilingual speech interpreters are continued at present.

All these elaborations are based on the modeling of human intellectual activity and on the constructive analysis of digital information by means of its synthesis. The method that is used is recognized around the world.

- Algorithmic analysis of the deep language structures. Attempts to create systems of artificial intelligence demand the deep analyses of historical roots and evolution of language structures and human cognition processes. Such analysis has been done using new algorithmic methods ,3 . The kernel recursive structure of language sentences and literature constructions have been revealed. The algorithmic model of language constructions invariant to the natural languages has been suggested. The practical results of this research include applications to the authorship problem, psycholinguistics, associative expert systems, analyzes of myths, multilingual translators and some others.

- Automatic forming and translation of keywords in querying systems. In the navigating the multilingual Internet the problem of adequate translation of keywords is of great importance. The direct translation of keywords from a language A to a language B is connected with high ambiguity and can complicate the search of necessary documents. More correct idea to the keywords translation is based on the comparison of texts in the language A, which correspond to the given set of keywords, with texts in the language B which could be found by means of all variants of translations of the given key-word set. In the process of looking for similarity of keywords an neural network model could be used.

The neural network methodology for implementation of this method has been elaborated. The methodology was checked in the automatic detection of user's interests.

These principles formed the base for creating neural networks supporting processes of making decisions and pattern recognition. Particularly, works in handwritten symbols neural recognition have been started with the Japanese company WACOM and at present gives good results. The same results could be used in the multilingual Internet.

- Multilingual Internet and Educational Problems. Multilingual Internet is thus becoming a real need for the nearest future, and important and urgent efforts should be made to solve the global problem of bi-directional communication barriers on different levels, addressing different user groups, etc. At the same time, due to low experience of the new users in the language and telematics, additional measures should be undertaken to provide training and educational facilities for these users.

Ukraine (and some CIS countries) can be considered as a typical "country in transition" concerning production, dissemination and use of multilingual information on the global information highways. There is an urgent need to develop an effective infrastructure in the field and to adjust to international standards. On the other hand, it is ready for international co-operative projects, having know-how and qualified specialists in many fields, including computer science, linguistics, programming, education, etc. Currently the following directions are considered as a first priorities in the National Informatization Programme: Basics in Telematics (Internet), networking of information and educational resources and multilingual computer-based support in science, education and communication, creation of the distance education centre.

Our preliminary analysis shows that the CIS countries have serious needs in the field of multilingual telematics support. Russian and French-speaking users are very conscious that they waste too much time and loose essential context information when they read/write texts in another language, even if they are competent in it. To keep one language such as English as unique language of communication is not cost-effective. There is a strong desire to stay within own native languages, which does not of course except trying to learn a few others for personal communicational and cultural purposes.

The following specific multilingual user's needs are:

- support of communication at the basic level (reading and writing) via e-mail;
- opprtunities to use the adequate e-mail packages to remove essential obstacles in the way of communication both in countries, and in international communication;
- analysis of the multilingual products and services in Internet;

- analysis of the machine translators (on-line and off-line), dictionaries (on-line, off-line), thesauruses, multilingual mailers, tools for multilingual WWW-pages design, etc,
- training in multilingual Internet services (free distant courses via e-mail, WWW-courses etc.);
- updated information about new tendencies and products in multilingual telematics support;
- resolve the problems of standardization for multilingual software for every site in CIS countries;
- organization of the multilingual support of users' sites and consultation services.

The problems related to supporting user and/or suppliers groups and standardization becoming more and more actual both for East users and West suppliers. To make all relevant information available to its potential users and to provide an information exchange between Internet-users from various professional fields and from different countries, relevant national sites must be equipped by tools which form friendly and comfortable environment, making communication attractive for users world-wide, developing their information needs, widening their horizons and motivating their creativity.

To facilitate a world-wide exchange via Internet specific needs of the users from wide range of cultural settings should be analyzed and generalized to find an effective solution.

The general goals of the multilingual telematic support for education and training are the following:

1. to provide basic language tools for effective information exchange between Internet users from all

possible professional fields and different English/ French and Russian speaking countries;

2. to improve accessibility of the Internet-based information for non-English speaking users;
3. to facilitate utilization of educational and training materials available in English for the French- and Russian-speaking users as well as to ensure share of such materials available on the net of the French and Russian-speaking countries;
4. to ensure exchange of educational and training information within Russian- speaking users groups directly, without necessity to pass through English.

To achieve these goals, the interested in multilingual applications sites must be equipped with tools which form user-friendly and comfortable multilingual environment. Communication within Network must be made attractive for users world-wide, developing their information needs, widening their horizons and motivating their creativity and inter- communications. The necessity of linguistic support for multilingual communication, information search and acquisition requires the use of modern linguistic tools such as spelling and grammar checkers, dictionaries, thesauri, vocabularies, elements of automatic translation and, eventually, multimedia voice encoders and decoders. To achieve the main goals for CIS countries, the translation tools for English into Russian and Ukrainian will be used.

- Virtual University as the examples of the multilingual telematics support for education and training. The life-long education of the 21st century will be global from two perspectives: from a horizontal perspective, cultures are meeting each other on the surface of the globe, entering into creative encounters that will produce a international collective virtual educational environment; from a vertical perspective, they must maximise using the world knowledge's for organisation of international virtual educational environment in order to provide a stable and secure base for future development. on the national and international levels .

The general goals of the multilingual telematic support for education and training are the following:

1. to provide basic language tools for effective information exchange between Internet users from all possible professional fields and different English/ French and Russian speaking countries;
2. to improve accessibility of the Internet-based information for non-English speaking users;
3. to facilitate utilization of educational and training materials available in English for the French- and Russian-speaking users as well as to ensure share of such materials available on the net of the French and Russian-speaking countries;
4. to ensure exchange of educational and training information within Russian- speaking users groups directly, without necessity to pass through English.

These problems must be solved at local, regional, national and international levels. The global aims of the IVU "Ukraine" are the following:

1. to provide inter-cultural courses, accessible to students all over the world through distance learning methods.

2. to create multilingual learning environment for telematic-based education and training
3. to stimulate learning to creative candidates in order to form complete human beings with erudition.

The multilingual telematics support for education and training should be based on innovative ways for flexible integration of modern technologies into the new solutions directed to the development of multimedia learning environment, which in its turn will contribute to the introduction of innovative solutions and skills for telematics-based training in world society, promoting new opportunities for life-long distance education.

To facilitate a world-wide exchange within the Network its local/national sites should analyse specific needs of its users to find an effective solution within the Network. One of this specific needs is the necessity of language support for multi-lingual communication and exchange of materials. To facilitate the use of samples and examples from different sources the Network should support a communication between teachers, as well as material translation into native language. This language service within local sites would not only promote the use of English-based materials outside English-speaking countries but also open the gates to teachers experience in other cultures and languages.

The use of current machine translation tools, spell- and grammar-checkers, vocabularies would help to improve them making a necessary office tool, as text editor or word processor.

Multilingual Internet support development. Main research direction is methods development for multilingual Internet technologies teaching to insure intencive use of the modern infornation resourses by the different groups of people.

Working in Internet multilingual environment create a large amount of the problems for non-English speakers. Such users cannot to solve these problems allways self-sufficiently. Activity in this direction was initiated at Second International Congress UNESCO and was supported by the 42 counries round the world. Such developments are absent in Ukraine. However, there is strong need to overcome language barriers and ensure certain translation or explanation of terms are selected by the user. Besides that, there isn't any materials about language barriers overcoming, in spite of existing such experience for English, Dutch and French languages. For Russian and Ukrainian languages we have only American translation off-line centers. So this problem is actual for Ukraine, that only tries to occupy certain place among leading countries in telecommunication issues.

Object of investigation is ways of access to modern information Internet resourses with on-line and off-line electronic dictionaries and translators, and insuring flexible distance learning and providing measures, that will facilitate active use of the multilingual Internet environment.

Multilingualism: A Canadian Experience

Since its birth a generation ago, the Internet has been dominated by the English language and North American culture. In a 1998 survey conducted by the Internet research group, eMarketer, two-thirds (68 percent) of a little over 60 million Internet users worldwide reside in just two countries, the United States, with 37 million users, and Canada, which has just over 4 million. About 60 percent of the Internet host computers are located in the United States. Nine out of 10 Internet users today are English-speaking. No fewer than 82 percent of home pages (web sites) are in English, according to the Internet Society's survey of 60,000 computers with Internet addresses.

Yet some foresee an end to this electronic hegemony. The number of non-U.S. Internet users is about to outnumber those inside the country soon and increase by nine-fold over the next five years, from 16.4 million in 1997 to 143 million by the year 2002, representing an annual growth rate of 70 percent. In that case, the present practice of conducting business, presenting news and information, and performing discussion on the Internet will have to be drastically changed. The widespread use of English will eventually be contested and the Internet itself will become multicultural. This is already happening.

A consortium of American computer companies has developed a universal digital code known as Unicode to allow computers to represent the letters and characters of virtually all the world's languages.

Major search engines like Yahoo and Excite offer their services in multiple languages. Netscape Communications in partnership with the leading Latin American Internet service, Star Media Network, provides a free Internet guide in Spanish and Portuguese. Internet services in languages other than English, like Star Media, are starting to provide world and regional news, weather, stock listings, e-mail, chat rooms, Internet access and more, all in the users' native language.

Given such developments, optimists argue that far from ending diversity, the Internet will promote it by allowing even small groups of people to disseminate their messages worldwide. By overtaking the "middle range" languages, it may actually protect minority languages threatened with extinction. A wider range of languages on the Internet means at least in theory that a wider range of ideas will be exchanged in a cyberspace, the long-promised global village.

Despite a tremendous influx of non-English languages in recent years, however, the Internet has a long way to go before it becomes a truly multilingual medium. As long as English can be understood by the largest number of Internet users, the cyberspace will continue to be dominated by English as the primary language for international discourse and commerce, European languages as a tool for regional and specialized communication, and many other minor languages for local communication.

At a glance there is an advantage to having one language dominant in the cyberspace. In a world of five to eight thousand different ethnic groups who reside in approximately 160 nation states speaking 5,000 distinct languages, some language must be the common language of the Internet. Many people believe that English must be by default the standard language on the Internet, much as it is the international language of aviation. At present there are clear indications of English becoming a lingua franca in the cyberspace.

The Internet, the network of networks, is most likely to be governed by the logic of the "Metcalfe's Law," the so-called magic of interconnections. Connect any number of machines, 'n', whether computers, phones or even cars, and you get 'n' squared in exponential value. Simply put, the values of the interconnected entities increase exponentially. To expand this logic further, as English-speaking countries have happened to take the central role in world politics and economy in modern period (namely, Pax Britannica and Pax Americana), the English language will deepen its hold on the world as more people go on line.

As a recent British Council report shows, the evolution of the English language accelerates as it spreads beyond Anglo-Saxonism. The critical mass of English amongst providers and users is likely to drive the usage inexorably towards monoglot English. Even the French, famously fastidious abcut guarding their language against dilution by foreign words and phrases, has been forced to surrender to American vernacular on Internet matters.

As English continues to dominate the cyberspace with greater intensity and speed, global resistance to it accelerates with equal strength. Some countries already disgruntled by the encroachment of the American culture—from pop music, blue jeans, to videos—are worried that their cultures will be further eroded by an American dominance in the cyberspace. In their minds, English, by association, immediately evokes a negative image of colonial imperialism.

They feel that it may threaten their cultures, their languages, even identities. For this ideological reason, many people in the Third World countries are opposed to having English as the lingua franca for commerce and trade, crisis management, and scholarly and intellectual discourse on the Internet. While the Internet is awash in information, almost all of it flows in one direction, i.e., from the United Sates to the rest of the increasingly wired world. It brings home the age-old controversy regarding unbalanced and unidirectional flow of information from the world's richest countries to the Third World, an on-going controversy that prompted UNESCO to declare a New World Information Order (NWIO) on several occasions.

For the ideological as well as practical purposes, many countries have taken steps to protect the Internet from excessive American influence. The French government once filed a lawsuit against a Georgia Tech campus in Metz, France, whose web page did not translate its contents into French. Arab countries proposed creation of an Arab Intranet, a closed network in which indiscriminate access to pornography and political discussion could be blocked. Canadian content requirements are to be extended to the Internet to keep out the American "cultural vulture."

Multilingualism: A Korean Experience

American culture has continued to exert its influence in Korea, first through Christian missions, trade and Hollywood productions, and more recently via the Internet. Thanks to the Korean government's aggressive drive, an estimated 2.5 million Koreans are linked to the global medium. An equally large share of the credit for the phenomenal growth of the Internet goes to the media organizations in Korea, which have in recent years vigorously campaigned for introducing the "Net" to the school community through such programs as the KidNet (Chosun Ilbo) and Internet in Education (Joongang Ilbo).

In the vicissitudes of hopes and fears about the Internet, two isolated but interrelated events recently took place in Korea, all with a nationalistic overtone. One is the Microsoft's abortive attempt to buy out a local Korean software company in exchange for a multi-million dollar investment. The other has to do with a somewhat radical proposal by a Korean writer to adopt English as a common language on the Internet.

In the midst of currency crisis in Korea these days came the shocking announcement that the Hangul and Computer (H&C) Company, a Korean software company, had agreed with Microsoft to stop development of its popular Arae A Hangul word processor program in exchange for a $20 million capital investment. Apparently, what Microsoft hoped for in the deal was to secure a monopolistic right of its Korean language version of Windows and Word in the Korean market. When it first appeared in 1990, Arae A Hangul-- named after the Korean alphabet invented by King Sejong more than five centuries ago--was the only word processor based on hangul instead of Roman letters with the hangul mapping.

Arae A Hangul, "insanely great" in the words of Apple Computer's founder Steven Jobs, was multilingual at a time when DOS versions of Word and WordPerfect barely went beyond ASCII. This made it easy to develop a number of attractive fonts frequently used in displaying old Korean characters.

Media reports of the deal aroused anger and frustration among Korean computer users and non-users alike. Defenders of Hangul, who were opposed to the Microsoft's planned equity participation in H&C, quickly invoked the issue of Korean national pride to rally the public support for the program. A massive nationwide campaign saved Hangul at the eleventh hour from the threat of extinction as its developer, H&C, reversed its earlier decision to sell off the software, bowing to a nationwide campaign spearheaded by Korean scholarly community and venture capitalists. As hindsight, invoking Korean pride as a defense against predatory foreign companies appears to be too far-fetched and even xenophobic. On the other hand, Microsoft's aggressive marketing strategy to effectively terminate H&C's further development of Hangul can be viewed as too selfish and insensitive to the Korean nationalistic sentiment.

Now that 2.5 millions of Koreans are linked up to form a global community, how will they communicate? Majority of Korean Internet users was found to use the global medium mainly for communication within the national boundary, according to an Internet user survey. To most of them the Internet remains largely an unexplored reservoir of knowledge and information due to language barrier.

Their grasp of English is quite rudimentary, sufficient only for processing basic information such as the weather, sports, and erotic visuals. Only a fraction of the Internet users can, to whatever degree, comprehend and produce written or spoken utterances in English. As a result, they are denied of the tremendous opportunities that the Internet has to offer, namely, in-depth information and more serious discussions with the netizens all around the world. To be an effective Internet user one has to be equipped with both receptive and productive abilities in English. Such an expectation, however, appears to be neither practical nor realistic as far as Korea is concerned.

Bok Koh-Ill, a professional Korean writer, thinks otherwise. He came up with a radical idea to make English as an official language of Korea along with Korean. Touching on the sensitive theme of Korean nationalism, Bok argued that "putting 'emotional' nationalism under control is not enough." "As the world is rapidly moving toward a Terrestrial Empire," he further asserted, "not only the political supranational organizations such as the WTO and IMF but also the communication tools like the Internet are increasingly integrated into one unity."

Now comes his argument concerning English, the dominant language on the Internet. Bok observed that "the emergence of the universal language is interlocked with the enlargement of network." He predicted that "the Korean language will soon be little more than a museum piece as more nations will adopt a bilingual system in which their own languages coexist with English." His underlying perspective about language is that "language is a tool, and worshipping it as an idol is irrational."

Sensationalism notwithstanding, Bok's audacious proposal immediately touched off a flurry of verbal battle between the conservatives and liberals in Korea. In a wild exchange of high-pitched diatribes, Bok's opponents argued that English was not panacea and accepting his idea would wither Korea's unique traditions and hamstring the very cultural foundation.

Bok's supporters applauded accuracy of his observation that Koreans possess an excessive national pride, which Bok sees as the obstacle to the advancement of the Korean society. Bok even dared all his critics by asking, "If you had to choose between English and Korean for your child's native language, which one would you select? If you choose English, your child is sure to have faster access to cutting-edge technology and information. If the Korean language is your choice, your child is doomed to lag behind in competition with others."

Whether he will succeed in his effort is far from certain. Bok says, "In our society, nationalism and national language are far too sensitive issues to be discussed with composure." Yet his other key point—that Koreans are too sensitive to these kinds of issues—seems not that far from reality. A non-random online survey taken immediately after the verbal battle showed 58 percent of those polled were against Bok. Even more noteworthy is the fact that as high as 42 percent sided with Bok and his idea. The deepening dispute seems here to stay, at least for a while.

Multilingual Translation

For a truly multilingual Internet, the long-promised global village, to come of age, there are a host of difficult hurdles to overcome, including, among the many, technical difficulties of communicating in the majority of the world's languages and development of hardware and software for machine-aided translations. Some progress has been made, and more in sight, in the development of hardware and software for processing texts, from seven-bit ASCII to ISO-Latin, and more recently, to Unicode (ISO 10646), a coding scheme for characters of most of the world's scripts.

Widely hailed as a significant breakthrough in electronic communication worldwide, Unicode character encoding, however, may not be the best one to use in our environment. For example, the Software Laboratory of Nippon Telegraph and Telephone Corporation (NTT) found that Chinese, Japanese, and Korean (CJK) ideographs share the same code space, when Unicode is used in a global search-engine context. Thus, if a Japanese searcher inputs a string for searching, it can equally match against Chinese and Korean counterparts. Another major problem with Unicode for CJK users is that it doesn't contain enough code space to capture all ideographs. For the development of a perfect multilingual architecture, incorporating languages that build compound characters or right-to-left ordering needs further tests.

Transmitting a message in a language of reader's preference is one thing; one's ability to comprehend it is quite another. In order to send and receive a message, most readers will have to rely on human translators/ interpreters. The Internet is home to many language translation sites that offer everything from simple online dictionaries to e-mailed translation services. From the desktop, one can request a translation by selecting to pay for human translation.

The global nature of the Internet has proved a boon to translation services, such as TAR Communication in New York, which translated Web-based press releases into 28 languages during the Atlanta Olympic Games in 1996. Translation business via the Internet within the next five years is expected to account for 30 percent of their work.

Given the volume and variety of messages on the Internet, however, exclusive reliance on human translation appears to be an unrealistic proposition. It is too slow and costly to make it a sensible choice for maintaining multilingual websites. A viable alternative is machine-aided translation, which has been vigorously pursued mostly in Japan, Canada and Europe with somewhat mixed results. Systran, available on the French Minitel network since 1983 and Canada's Meteo system, which translates meteorological bulletins between French and English, are considered to be success stories.

In Korea there are several translation softwares capable of machine-translating foreign language texts into Korean. In an attempt to assess the quality of these softwares, the author had a wide variety of texts in Japanese and English translated into Korean by means of King Sejong, one of the most popular translation softwares in the market.

To begin with a conclusion, the Japanese-Korean translation effort proved to be a resounding success, whereas the translated version of the English texts was dismally unsatisfactory. In terms of the syntax and grammar both Korean and Japanese share a lot of things in common, whereas there is a mile of difference between Korean and English. It seemed as if the intercultural difference involved in the English-Korean translation were an insurmountable wall indeed.

The English texts included Abraham Lincoln's Gettysburg address, a *USA Today* article headlined "White House Loses Round in Lindsey Case," a passage in Jean Baudrillard's La Pensee Radicale, excerpts from the novel Little Prince, and a paragraph in Nico Randeraad's article "Authority in Search of Liberty." This mini exercise yielded disconcertingly unsatisfactory results.

The translated versions were totally unintelligible, and not good enough to be revisable even with the intervention of human editors. It appeared that the texts replete with sophisticated literary expressions—the Lincoln's address and Baudrillard's work in particular—simply defied machine-aided translation. Of the five different kinds of the English texts, only the *USA Today* article—concerning a U. S. court's refusal of the White House appeal to block prosecutors from questioning a presidential aide about Monica Lewinsky--showed some sign of hope. Compared with the other texts, the news article revealed a relatively high level of fidelity in translation.

Why did the newspaper article alone fare reasonably well, while other texts simply failed to be translated into Korean? The translator's familiarity with the subject matter, i.e. President Clinton's sex scandal, could be an important factor. A more plausible explanation lies in the journalistic style in which the article is written. Journalists are required to adhere to the journalistic principle of brevity and precision when they write about an issue or event. All the important elements are to be clearly spelled without excessive literary ornamentation.

Such a finding could have a practical implication for the information producers on the Internet. For the benefit of a large number of population worldwide they are strongly encouraged to provide a brief and concise abstract of the full text in a machine-friendly manner, so that the abstract can be translated into many languages without losing fidelity.

Also useful in multilingual translation will be a two-step process now being implemented by several groups including the United Nations University in Tokyo. In the two-step process, a text is first thoroughly analyzed into component parts (title, paragraph, sentence), clarified when necessary and possible by a dialogue with the author, then translated into an intermediate, abstract representation—which is used to generate translations in different languages. In this way, readers who have no receptive ability in a foreign language could at least get the gist of the material in hand with the help of translation softwares.

Human-assisted Machine Translation

Given the low quality of machine translation and the expensive nature of human translation, the only logical option available to Korea--and for that matter to many countries in the world--appears to be human-assisted/ validated machine translation. Experts at numerous regional and international conferences have already addressed to the crucial importance of human-assisted translation. To briefly summarize their recommendations and suggestions:

1) it is vital that a human validator is used to correct automatic translation;
2) it is important to take cultural-specific notions into account when undertaking translations between culturally different linguistic areas;
3) human translations can benefit from processing of files against terminology databases to ensure that technical phrases are translated in a domain-specific way;
4) as keyword matching does not work across domains or across languages, searchable concept-based terminology resources and thesauri are needed;

5) it is important to integrate machine translation and domain-specific terminology sets with authoring tools to speed up translation services.

Technological solution to machine translation is one thing, financial difficulty associated with making machine translation services available through the Internet is another. Because these services take up too many CPU cycles, Information Service Providers would rather offer these services via specialist servers, not as a part of their mainstream operations.

The question then arises as to who pays for such servers, and how. Also, the preponderance of English on the Web, with some estimates ranging as high as 95%, appears at odds with the huge investments in translation to be made by the software industry. Investments are likely to be made in the cost-effective European languages, but not in minor languages.

Preparing for the multilingual Internet calls for a concerted effort by both public institutions and industry players that produce and utilize language services, tools, and systems. Regional cooperation among nations that share cultural and linguistic similarities, such as Korea, Japan, and China, must be strongly encouraged not only by the governments concerned but also by regional and international organizations such as UNESCO. Through collaborative R&D arrangements, they can jointly develop multilingual translation tools and services in a much more cost-effective way.

From ephemeral to robust cyber community

As personal computers become less expensive and user-friendlier, people outside North America and European countries are becoming increasingly linked. In this atmosphere diversity of languages will further enrich the on-line environment by making it possible for people of different cultures and languages to engage themselves in more serious in-depth discussions with other people. There are many advantages of a multilingual Internet: it would allow much more effective and wide diffusion of information and knowledge than would otherwise be possible; common mistakes and misunderstandings resulting from language barrier will be curtailed; and it could be a crack in Americana hegemony over Internet culture.

A multicultural and multilingual Internet has the potential to be simultaneously more universalistic and more particularistic, more global and more local, more cosmopolitan and more parochial, and more mass-oriented and more elite-oriented. The cybersociety created by the Internet as we know it today is drawn heavily from the rich and educated in the rich countries. By appearing to be global and universalistic, the Internet masks its very particular and elite characteristics. If it were allowed to continue to develop the way it had been, the global medium would fall a victim to its own success by further benefiting the rich and well-educated at the cost of the underprivileged.

The Web is an ephemeral community, to borrow words from Jim Falk, which is "unstable and transitory." "Relationships within an ephemeral community, whether emotional or intellectual, are likely to be partial, satisfying only one or a few of the members' needs." In contrast, Falk maintains, a robust community is one in which "the members have not only a sense of interrelatedness and shared experience, but also share common ideals and believe that through by virtue of belonging to their community they can make great progress towards achieving their objectives than through belonging to other communities. Members will invest personal resources, energy and commitment into it because they consider it stable, growing, supportive and effective." Multilingualism on the Internet is a necessary, if not the sufficient, condition for transforming an ephemeral cybersociety into a robust one.

8

Rural Accessibility

More than 2.5 billion people—over 40% of the planet's population—live in rural and remote areas of developing countries. Of the small fraction that have any access to telecommunications, radio broadcast and voice telephony have traditionally been the main services provided. Today, a wide variety of new services such as e-mail, e-commerce, tele-education, tele-health/tele-medicine, among others, has made access to interactive multimedia services as important for rural and remote communities as voice connectivity alone.

Since each district or community requires a different mix of voice text, image, video and audio communications to best meet its needs, today's telecommunications network operators must be able to support a range of services and bandwidth levels at a reasonable cost. Rural and remote areas exhibit one or more of the following characteristics:

— scarcity of absence of public facilities such as reliable electricity supply, water, access roads and regular transport;

— scarcity of technical personnel

— difficult topographical conditions, e.g. lakes, rivers, hills, mountains or desserts which render the construction of telecommunications networks very costly

— severe climatic conditions that make critical demands on the equipment

— low level of economic activity mainly based on agriculture, fishing, handicrafts, etc.;

— low per capita income

— underdeveloped social infrastructure(health, education, etc):

— low population density;

— very high calling rates per exchange line, reflecting the scarcity of telephone service and the fact that large numbers of people rely on a single exchange line.

These characteristics make it difficult to provide public telecommunications services of acceptable quality by traditional means at affordable prices, while also achieving commercial viability for the service provider.

After the extensive research through its web site, ITU's Focus Group on new technologies for rural applications, recently issued the report on a wide and ever increasing array of low cost information and communications technologies and solutions capable of supporting sustainable and socially beneficial services for rural areas.

Fifteen years before the concept of digital divide was acknowledged, Independent Commission for World Wide

Telecommunication Development, chaired by Sir Donald Maitland set a goal in its report known by the title "The Missing Link" to bring telephone services within easy reach of all human kind. Basic recommendations of the Maitland Commission are still worth revisited when the subject of bridging the gaps or rural access is addressed.

Valleta Action Plan(VAP), formulated at the second World Telecommunication Development Conference in Malta, March 1998 sought to promote universal access to basic telecommunication, broadcasting and Internet as tools for development in rural areas. Focus Group on topic 7 "new technologies for rural application" which was established later in one of Study Groups of ITU-D started its activities from June, 1999.

A round table on rural access was organized by the initiative of Focus Group 7 during the ITU's AMERICAS TELECOM2000 in Rio de Janeiro which was participated by the rural telecommunication operators and regulators of the region.

The round table discussion provided us valuable information regarding the profitability of rural and remote telecommunications in Latin American countries. The activities such as collection of case reports and the on line discussion were conducted mainly on the web site and the final report were accomplished based on the analysis of the collected case reports which are available now in three languages.

ITU's web site was established to gather information on the development of telecommunication technologies that truly meet the needs of rural areas of developing and developed countries. The web site is a means of input for not only the ITU membership but also other organizations and individuals connected with developing rural areas through telecommunication. The virtual conference room and the contact information allowed direct contact with the authors of input. Three types of information were targeted.

a) ongoing projects using technologies specially designed for rural areas of developing countries including Multipurpose Community Tele-center, Telemedicine and Tele-education;

b) planned projects that make new combinations linked with WLL networks;

c) examples of how equipment has been adapted for use in particular, harsh climatic or other conditions of remote and rural areas, such as solar powered telephone

Based on the data gathered through the web site, Focus Group aimed,

a) to select those types of project or system that have social or economic importance but limited commercial profitability, so that the ITU can focus special support upon such projects in helping to develop technology for rural applications;

b) to list new measures to be taken by ITU-D to encourage manufacturers and relevant organizations to create technology tailored to developing countries;

c) among those measure, to recommend priorities that ITU-D should follow to help achieve the development of technology for rural applications.

57 reports were collected in the case library of the web site by the time to draft the final report of the Focus Group 7 which were deemed appropriate considering the quality and quantity of the information contained in the report.

Rural areas can generally characterized by low population density and long distances between settlement areas. Due to unfavorable geographic and climatic conditions, access from urban centers to rural areas, and vice versa, is often difficult. Further disadvantage of rural areas are:

a) Low educational level, high illiteracy rate

b) Hardly any job opportunities

c) Low income per capita and per family

d) Increasing migration of the young to urban centers

e) Unreliable and badly functioning public transport

f) Irregular, if any, power supply

g) Poor health care and medical services

h) Lack of other government services

i) Little participation in national affairs

The basic objectives to which telecommunications services have to contribute are to trigger and sustain structural and economic development, to eliminate the above mentioned disadvantages and to generally improve the quality of life in rural and remote areas.

Annual public expenditure on health and education in the world's low income countries is estimated at more than U$100 billion. Where the cost and/or outcomes of these expenditures can be improved through the use of telecommunications, access to appropriate infrastructure becomes not only a human right, but a financial necessity. New industries and other commercial operations are attracted only to places where telecommunications are at hand.

Unserved rural areas will, therefore, develop only slowly, if at all, thus contributing to the acceleration of unwanted rural to urban migration. One of several preconditions to reverse this trend is the availability of telecommunication services.

Other benefits of telecommunications concern security, the elimination of feeling of isolation and insecurity in rural villages as well as improvement of government administration. Public administration becomes more effective with telecommunications because it relies heavily on ordination between central headquarters, regional and local offices as well as individual government officers in outlying districts.

It has turned out, though, that the full impact of improved telecommunications comes only to bear if road conditions are also improved. Many of the most critical factors that enable rural areas to benefit from technology lie beyond the network and its elements. Sustainable business models, political will, skills training and education are just as critical - if not more so - than selecting the most appropriate technology fiom among a range of reasonable alternatives

The Focus Group found out that the Internet is the most widely used plat form adopted to deliver multimedia applications in rural areas of developing countries. While much negative attention in developing countries has been focused on the use of the Internet as illegal bypass mechanism in the international traffic arena, the long term importance of the Internet for developing countries lies in its potential to improve the domestic flow of economic and educational resources between isolated rural communities and urban centers. Areas of application for Internet and other communication based services include telemedicine and public health education, coordinating regional food security efforts, making government sponsored agricultural extension services more effective and accessible to rural farmers, and enabling more rural children, adolescents and post-secondary students to receive education, among others.

Communication based applications are being designed and implemented in rural areas of developing countries by a wide variety of actors in addition to public telecommunication operators (PTO's). A significant portion of the expertise required to develop sustainable, connectivity-enabled applications for rural areas is located within the professional, academic, business and agricultural sectors, among others.

Not only to schools, universities, government departments, international organizations and NGOs routinely design and implement customized applications, they also independently purchase and set up information technology equipment. As a result, public telecommunications operators are increasingly required to support a heterogeneous mixture of networks, protocols and bandwidth requirements away from urban centers.

The need for basic literacy, computer skills and training in the use of ICT applications remains a significant challenge for rural areas. Language barriers and the complexity of personal computer operation have been shown to hinder Internet diffusion. Many innovative schemes have been devised in rural areas to overcome these barriers. Although not widely utilized, technique such as voice mail, translation of content, and icon based telephones indicate that foreign languages and illiteracy are not necessarily barriers to the use of communications services, if the end user's needs are comprehended and addressed. Relevant content is extremely critical to the success of any rural application.

A great deal of progress is being made in rural community and business development through the introduction of telephony, e-mail, tele-centers, and radio broadcasts. For example, infoDev-sponsored organization named PeopLink has established an e-commerce program allowing local artisans in developing countries to bypass middlemen and market their products directly to first world consumers. Two of the key requirements for the success of community and business development applications were found to be local language support and availability of relevant content.

The motivation and commitment to telemedicine in developing countries is very strong. This motivation is often backed by a willingness to pay for systems which are expected to improve health outcomes and lower medical costs in the long run. Telemedicine services may be perceived as more of necessity in developing countries than they are in the industrialized countries, resulting in a greater willingness among the former to change established methods of doctor-patient interaction and health care administration.

Telemedicine and healthcare applications are not limited exclusively to expensive, high bandwidth services. As long as the local medical community remains motivated and committed to implementing telemedicine and tele-health programs, there are a wide range of health benefits that can be achieved through remote patient monitoring and diagnosis, multimedia communication links between urban and remote facilities, and broadcast of health information over radio and television.

Unsurprisingly, the Focus Group found that university-level distance education program lend themselves to cross-border implementation. Using distribution by satellite or Internet, the administrative costs of running distance education courses can be spread over a very wide potential student base. A number of existing programs, such as the African Virtual University (AVU) and the distance education network of the University of the South Pacific(USPNet), are already based on the concept of cross-border educational access.

Problems with installation and maintenance of copper cable plant have prompted the widespread use of wireless systems in rural areas. Ten types of wireless access systems were identified through the case studies and ITU activities, illustrating existing and emerging access options for reaching rural communities. Given the trend toward shared facilities such as tele-centers, university extension centers, post office kiosks, etc., as well as the variety of revenue models associated with social services in the health, educational and e-commerce fields, the Focus Group considered technologies which expanded the number of supportable applications as well as those which demonstrated lower per-line costs.

Access options on the horizon for rural areas include a number of technologies that are new to the rural marketplace or still under development.

GSM cellular base stations implemented in the 400 MHz band are scheduled for commercial introduction in 2001. The use of the lower frequency band will enable each GSM 400 base station to cover approximately double the area achieved by existing GSM 900 base stations.

Third generation cellular systems, known as IMT-2000, are designed to deliver a wide range of traffic types more efficiently and inexpensively than the current generation of wired and cellular telephony networks. The World Administrative Radio Conference-2000 (WARC-2000) designated bands under 1 GHz in order to allow longer-range IMT-2000 cell sites, particularly for rural areas of developing countries. However, there are no firm indications from manufacturers about when commercial IMT-2000 systems using under 1 GHz will appear on the market.

Gateways based on ITU-T Recommendation H.323 support real-time, two-way communications between local area networks (LANs) and the PSTN. Such gateways offer developing countries the option of constructing local and wide area networks to deliver telephony and other services in rural areas, without undermining existing investments in the PSTN.

Demand for Internet-based services in rural areas, particularly email, has resulted in new applications of old technologies, such as VHF radio systems and meteor burst communications, for non-real time services. In addition, new combinations of existing technologies are extending the reach and flexibility of wireless access systems, as well as reducing total costs through the integration of shared systems and components. In particular, many rural operators are deploying very small aperture terminals (VSATs) and point-to-multipoint radio systems integrated with wireless local loop systems based on regional standards such as PHS and DECT.

Wireless router networks, integrated with IP telephony software, have the potential to provide significant cost savings and social benefits as multiservice platforms for tele-centers, government offices, schools and other organizations in rural areas. Since these technologies are largely untested in rural areas, Focus Group recommends that BDT conduct pilot projects aimed at confirming the technologies' robustness in rural environments and effectiveness in dealing with multimedia applications such as telemedicine, distance learning and so forth.

It is of the utmost importance that ITU-D strive to raise awareness of the rural information and communication needs of developing countries within the computing and information technology industry. Unlike the telecommunications industry, which has been doing business in underdeveloped rural areas for several decades, companies in the IT sector are generally unfamiliar with the environmental and social requirements of rural areas of developing countries.

Multimedia systems profiled by Focus Group 7, some of which were only launched during the period in which the report was written between June and August 2000, demonstrate many features with potential lifetime cost savings for rural areas.

For example, information appliances supporting email, World Wide Web (WWW) browsing and e-commerce applications provide simplified user interfaces in packages with fewer maintenance requirements than traditional PCs.

Internet client network solutions can offer Internet service providers (ISPs) the ability to upgrade their rural customers' browser and applications software remotely, reducing the skills requirements for tele-center operators and rural schools. Finally, technical institutes and R&D

organizations in developing countries such as India and Indonesia are developing their own custom, low cost IT terminals and devices.

The lack of mains energy supply in many rural and remote areas is a major obstacle to deploying telecommunication infrastructure. Many governments, agencies, and NGOs are currently working to support broader or massive use of telecommunications and IT systems in unelectrified rural areas. As a result, Focus Group 7 recommends that governments, administrations and recognized operating agencies consider closely linking renewable energy specialists with rural telecommunication and ICT initiatives.

In the past two decades, the most important use of renewable energy and hybrid systems in telecommunications has been for off-grid telecom repeaters. Due to the high cost of the repeater equipment, the critical role the repeaters play in the larger telecom networks, and the unattended nature of the systems, these power systems have been very carefully sized and designed using highly capable and experienced engineers. In contrast, the power requirements for user-side installations -- such as wireless local loop terminals, PCs and cellular handsets -- are relatively small. For such user-side equipment it will generally not be possible to rely upon the same approach to power system design as has been used for telecom repeater systems. Therefore, Focus Group 7 recommends that ITU-D support the efforts of the international renewable energy community by disseminating practical and useful information on small power systems for rural telecommunication installations to ITU-D members, project partners and other organizations.

Followings are the important elements for designing ICTs for rural areas of developing countries.

a) Use of wireless technologies for local loop network connecting the customers to the nearest local exchange or network node;

b) Implementation in low frequency bands for the wireless systems in sparsely populated rural areas (typically under 1GHz);

c) Modularity and scalability to meet the demand for services in rural areas where the network may be built out as needed and at the lowest incremental cost;

d) Remote network management for minimizing the operation and maintenance costs of rural installations;

e) Simplified user terminal configuration and operation for rural communities where they often lack the technical skills needed to install, configure and upgrade software on a typical personal computer;

f) Flexible user interface design with interfaces based on the input and output mechanisms such as icons, voice-oriented instructions, and choice of language and text.

g) Long life cycles for equipment for rural use which will take at least three years to recover investment, and some much longer than that;

h) Multi-user terminals for the shared use at multi-purpose community tele-centers with metering function, software to manage multiple users and other specialized payment and billing systems

i) Standard compliance of the equipment for rural use which conforms to standards of ITU and other recognized standard bodies;

j) Low power requirements which are critical in the rural areas.

There remain now some barriers in questions.

a) Frequencies under 1GHz are the suitable bands for the use of mobile services, and WLL in rural areas however there are services assigned to these bands in each countries. Frequency use for the rural services should be carefully investigated in close collaboration with the regional and national radio frequency authorities;

b) Frequency license fee are the remarkably augmented in some countries where the frequency auction methodology is implemented which will have implications to the increase of end user fee in the long run. There is the other option of so called "beauty contest" methodology without such implications. Which way to be followed by the developing countries will have consequential implications;

c) Regarding the Internet services, cost sharing of international Internet access line is under debate in regional and international meetings such as APEC, ITU-T, and WTSA (World Telecommunication Standard Assembly). US position and that of the rest of countries are in major contrast. The present status is that the latter is bearing the international access capacity to the former. APEC conducted the extensive research (ICAIS project) by outsourcing the research to a consultant about the historical background, internet traffic analysis, and network cost structures etc. and resulted in the compromised wording at Cancun, Mexico in May, 2000, that this matter should be for the private business arrangements and commercially negotiated but that the arrangements should reflect ideas of fairness. ITU-T and WTSA debated the recommendation of cost sharing concept and adopted with reservation by the US. Cost implications for Internet user calculated and claimed by an APEC country is U$40/year/user. Debate and the research are still under way in APEC and ITU.

The new goal was set by the Secretary General of the ITU during the opening of TELECOM99 last October while Mr. Kofi Annan, the Secretary General of the United Nation was attending; i.e. "to bring internet services to all humankind within a decade in the new millennium, and apply all the new technologies and impulses so that the gaps in connectivity to the Internet can be reduced".

To meet this goal, followings are the possible solutions for providing services to rural areas:

a) Wireless access systems such as FWA (Fixed Wireless Access) and VSAT are effective means of establishing infrastructure in rural areas since they are less costly and easier for installation over the wired systems;

b) IP(Internet Protocol) based network is more economical and flexible than circuit switched network;

c) Packet based wireless access technologies such as IMT-2000 and wireless routers, are being designed to deliver wide range of traffic types more efficiently than traditional wired and cellular telephony network;

d) Linking suppliers and implementers on the web by providing the comprehensive catalogue with contact information is the useful means for the equipment procurement with less cost;

e) Shared use concept is useful for making ICT terminals and facilities at Multipurpose Community Tele-centers available at affordable cost in rural users;

f) The financing scheme and/or special funding mechanism for the start-up of the rural and remote area services may be useful for the accelerated improvement of the rural and remote accessibility;

g) Collaboration for promotion of rural projects among multi-actors such as Governments, UN Agencies, PTOs and NGOs etc. should be encouraged.

h) Participation of women and the youth for the promotion of information access for rural community also be encouraged.

9

Management Information Systems

Management information systems (MIS) are fundamental for public sector organisations seeking to support the work of managers. Yet they are often ignored in the rush to focus on 'sexier' applications. This chapter aims to redress the balance by providing a detailed analysis of public sector MIS. It firstly locates MIS within the broader management monitoring and control systems that they support.

Understanding the broader systems and the relationship to public sector inputs, processes, outputs and outcomes is essential to understanding MIS. The chapter details the different types of reports that MIS produce, and uses this as the basis for an MIS model and a description of the decision-making benefits that computerised MIS can bring. Finally, the chapter describes generic public sector MIS that address internal government transactions, public administration/ regulation, and public service delivery. Real-world examples of all types are provided from the US, UK, Africa, and Asia.

Management information systems can be defined as information systems that provide reports which assist the managerial monitoring and control of organisational functions, resources or other responsibilities.

MIS were first developed during the 1950s and 1960s but came into the organisational mainstream somewhat later. There was a rich literature on MIS during the 1970s, continuing into the 1980s. However, the explosion of other organisational applications of IT has led MIS – at least as defined above – to retain only a small foothold in many more recent publications. Despite their book titles, for example, Hicks devotes just one chapter to MIS, whilst Laudon & Laudon devote just a few pages. Nonetheless the fundamental importance of MIS has meant some writers continue to provide a broad and deep discussion of the topic.

Our discussion in this chapter begins with a deeper understanding of the managerial processes that management information systems support.

Management Monitoring and Control Systems

This monitoring and control system consists of four main elements:

— *A process.* At the core of the system is some kind of process that turns inputs into outputs. Let us take the example of a public sector training project that seeks to provide new skills for the unemployed. This project turns inputs of money, equipment and staff labour into outputs of skilled people who are trained via processes of training delivery.

— *A monitoring mechanism:* This mechanism gathers information about the outputs from the process. For example, it would gather information about the number of people trained and the extent of their new skills in the training project.

— *A comparison mechanism:* This compares the information gathered about current performance with information on previously-set plans, benchmarks, targets, etc. These two types of information represent the information needs of the monitoring and control system. For example, this mechanism would compare information on actual skills gained with skill gain targets. This part of the system is often known as the 'evaluation mechanism' (as in the phrase, 'monitoring and evaluation').

— *A control mechanism:* This decides upon and then ensures implementation of corrective action based on the output of the comparison. For example, where skill levels produced by training were lower than expected, changes to the method or location of training might be decided upon and implemented.

Monitoring and control therefore represents a *feedback loop,* in which information about a later stage is fed back into control of an earlier stage. Where all is well, the system's only function is to monitor and report. Where a problem - a shortfall between the actual and the desired situation - arises, the system's function is to assess the impact of that problem, and to decide on and then implement remedial action. Most organisational systems are intended to work on a *negative feedback* principle where corrective action is in the opposite direction to monitored deviations from norms. Take the case of a budget system. Where the monitoring mechanism indicated that more than budget was being spent, feedback should lead the control mechanism to correct this by starting to spend less.

Rationally, the system provides the mechanisms by which the organisation a) knows if it is achieving its objectives, and b) achieves its objectives in the face of problems. In order for this to happen, all the following must be present:

— outputs that can be measured,

— a monitoring mechanism that does measure the outputs,

— a monitoring mechanism that produces information on the outputs that is accurate, timely, relevant, and complete,

— a comparison mechanism,

— targets against which to compare,

— a control and implementation mechanism, and

— an overall feedback loop that does not take too long to be effective.

MIS can be of two different types:

— *Monitoring MIS*: these MIS merely gather information about output performance and present it to the manager, who will then do the comparison him/herself.

— *Monitoring and comparison MIS*: for these MIS, the pre-set standards for output performance have been entered onto the computer system. The MIS is therefore able to perform the comparisons itself. This forms the basis of exception reporting, discussed below.

Computers are not a necessary part of this or any other management system. There are many manual methods of monitoring and comparing, such as:

— tables of accounts and budgets,

— a chart of staff names and absence days. or

— a line on the wall which, when reached by a diminishing pile of stock items, indicates that they should be re-ordered.

However, computerisation will be our focus in this chapter.

Complicating the Simple Picture

So far, a relatively simple picture has been presented of both management system and information system. However, there are four main ways in which these systems differ, as described next.

i. *What is monitored:* inputs, outputs and outcomes The model above places a process at the centre of the model. But, for many management information systems, the focus is on the measure being monitored and reported upon. In overall organisational terms, these measures are not always outputs, but can be divided into three categories:

— *Inputs*: the resources that are used by the organisation.

— *Outputs*: the direct services (or products) produced by the organisation.

— *Outcomes*: the wider impacts of organisational outputs.

To differentiate these, let us take the example of an enterprise development agency. Its inputs would include general financial expenditure and hours of staff time worked. Its outputs could include number of clients served, and number and size of loans provided or guaranteed. The outcomes could include number of new enterprises created, enterprise growth rates, number or proportion of people employed in enterprises, and average income per capita.

An MIS can monitor one or more of these measures. In the latter case, it will need some mechanism for integrating or at least co-ordinating the different measures.

ii. What is controlled: plans, inputs and processes: The control mechanism can focus on one or more different parts of the model:

— *Processes*: The training project example given above described control of processes.

— *Inputs*: Alternatively, information may be fed back further 'upstream' than processes, and affect the inputs to the process. For example, the information gathered on skill levels produced by the training project might indicate that, to generate the required outputs, altering the training method or location was not enough. Instead, more labour (e.g. a higher trainer:trainee ratio) or more investment (e.g. in better-paid, better-qualified trainers) was required.

— *Plans*: Moving even further 'upstream' in the model, information may be fed back to affect the original planning of the process. For example, the information gathered might indicate that no amount of 'tinkering' with inputs or methods can produce the originally-planned outputs. The plans themselves would therefore have to be amended. These changes could be directed at increasingly higher-order parts of planning:

- *Amended targets*: For example, revised output targets on the number of skilled trainees or the depth of required skills to be produced.

- *Amended immediate objectives*: For example, changing the project to produce a different set of skills.

- *Amended intermediate objectives*: For example, changing the project type from increasing the employability of the jobless through training to provision of a direct employment subsidy.

- *Amended overall objectives*: For example, changing from trying to raise employment levels in a poor rural district to encouraging relocation to areas of high employment demand.

iii. *Management role supported:* Management information systems can support the different management roles of public administration:

— *Operational management*: This role is often largely supervisory in nature and so MIS for operational management may well be used to support day-to-day monitoring and control. Such MIS will not contain 'higher-order' feedback to plans. These MIS might involve any of the areas in which basic operational information systems function such as accounting and human resources. As described below, systems supporting this type of role may be particularly appropriate for automation of control and decision making because of the relatively narrow, structured nature of the role. Sea Lake County Welfare Department in the US, for example, used an operational MIS to support the day-to-day monitoring and authorisation of food stamps and other welfare payments.

— *Tactical management*: MIS for this role operate in the same areas as for operational management, but take an organisationally-broader and longer-term perspective. There might be a greater emphasis on human decision making (because situations are less certain and structured) and on more 'upstream' control feedback. In the Sea Lake case, tactical MIS were used to monitor accumulated reasons for welfare denial, and for welfare case opening and closing.

— *Strategic management*: MIS can and do support strategic management. However, rational description of the strategic role places a particular emphasis on planning and, for more senior managers, on an integrated view of the organisation. This is seen as being supported mainly by executive information systems. In the Sea Lake case, the executive information system incorporated both internal welfare data and external data on government regulations to assist strategic planning.

iv. *Automation of control:* In many management information systems, the output from the comparison stage forms an input to human decision making. However, in some information systems the process of decision making may be automated. For example, inventory information systems can gather data on the level of stocks and suggest the decision that particular items should be re-ordered if stocks fall below a certain level. Some such systems even create the order form and send it electronically to a supplier.

Features of Management Information Systems

You should by now understand the main rationale for a management information system. In order to draw up a model of an MIS, two further elements must be described: the link to data-gathering systems and the production of reports.

MIS often rely on monitoring data produced by a corporate database. In many cases, the division between the two systems is not obvious. For example, many users merely perceive that they have a payroll system that collects payroll data, produces both operational payroll information and management reports, and is used for both operation and monitoring/control of the payroll system.

Central to its monitoring and control roles, an MIS produces reports. This is mainly what managers perceive about an MIS since these are its tangible outputs. Reports come in many forms, as described below. They can be differentiated in two main ways: by content and by schedule.

i. *Differentiation by content:* MIS reports fall into three main categories of content:

— *Detail report*. This contains all relevant information on the report topic. For example, a detailed payroll report might give the following information for all staff: employee number, name, wage/salary rate, standard monthly earnings, standard tax payable, and each individual monthly payment for the year to-date.

— *Summary report.* This contains a summarisation of information on the report topic. For example, the total number of staff in each unit, each unit's total payroll bill for this year and last year, and the percentage change between the two. Some summaries may be recognised performance indicators. For example, one measure of a unit's performance might be its total actual payroll bill as a proportion of the total budgeted payroll bill.

— *Exception report.* This filters out information to provide just that which is deemed to be most important, according to some pre-set criteria. It may be summarised or detailed. For example, a report could include employee name, total individual payroll payments this and last year, and percentage change between the two, only for those staff whose pay rose by more than 10 per cent.

These reports may find themselves combined. For example, a report might:

— provide information on unit salary and income tax payment totals (summary),

— for only those units where the total was more than 5 per cent above last year's total (exception), and

— allow the manager to break this down into individual staff salaries and tax payments if required (detail).

ii. *Differentiation by schedule* : MIS reports fall into three main categories of schedule:

— *Periodic report*: This is produced at regular intervals: daily, weekly, monthly, quarterly, etc. For example, a report of organisational unit salary totals produced every month after staff have been paid.

— *Event-triggered report*: This is produced in response to a particular event or set of conditions. An example of the former might be a detailed payroll report produced once the first tranche of federal government funding for a project was agreed. An example of the latter might be a detailed payroll report produced if the total payroll bill in a unit exceeded budget in any month by more than 3 per cent. In some cases, more than a report might be triggered. For instance, the last example could also trigger production of a pro forma memo to the head of unit warning them about their payroll expenditure situation.

— *Request report*: This is produced as and when required in response to an ad hoc request. For example, a payroll report on all staff in the top two salary grades could be produced in response to a politician's concern about increasing public vs. private sector pay differentials for top managers.

The Role of Reports

Periodic summary and detailed reports are the 'bread and butter' of management information systems. For certain older MIS, this might be all that they produced. However, it is the other forms of report that provide MIS with much of their organisational value. If they work correctly, for example, exception-triggered reports can take a substantial monitoring workload from managers. Managers know that the computer system is 'watching out' for certain problems and will alert them if these problems arise. Examples could include alerting reports when:

— an unusually large amount of cash is involved in a transaction,

— there is a sudden increase in recorded imports, or

— more than three states report the incidence of Colorado beetle infestation.

Reports with just exception contents provide no redundant information, but just focus the manager on problem areas that require corrective action. This therefore helps managers cope with the problem of information overload. Exception reports have a wide variety of applications and can provide, for example:

— just the names of those staff who have been absent more than five times during the past month,

— details of only those loans which have received no repayment for more than eight weeks, or

— codes of only those budget heads which are more than 10 per cent over-spent.

One exception report issue lies in the choice of exception condition on which to report. In the loan example, the eight week condition might be a bad choice. It could be that an eight week delay is perfectly normal. The report is therefore unnecessarily targeting many borrowers who are not in trouble. Alternatively, it could be that a default of only two weeks indicates that help is needed. By eight weeks, matters may have deteriorated too far for any outside assistance to be of value. There will have to be an input of both experience and analytical skills in the choice of exception condition.

A second exception report issue relates to data inputs: such reporting can only be relied upon if data inputs are being continuously and reliably gathered.

Request reports provide the manager with a great deal of power. They can produce information that more exactly matches the manager's particular needs at the moment of need. Request reports are often a response to the unexpected. Examples could include reports on:

— the finances of a project, for input to a meeting requested by the project manager,

— those clients who have been occupying a refuge bed for more than six months, in response to a shortage of beds for incoming homeless persons, or

— the past training of a staff member, in response to their request to go on a training course.

Typically these request reports are produced using search forms or search expressions. Many computerised management information systems allow this to be done online: the request is typed in and the report appears almost immediately on-screen. There will often be a choice of showing the report as a table of figures or, if appropriate, as a graph, or as both.

As with all information systems, the response to the request can only be as good as the data that has been put into the system. MIS data is often entered with the expected rather than the unexpected in mind, leading to the risk that unexpected requests cannot be answered. If, on the other hand, large swathes of data are entered into the MIS 'just in case they are needed', this runs the risk of substantial expenditure on gathering data that is never used. A balance should therefore be struck between the likelihood of needing data in a request plus the value of being able to respond to that request, and the cost of providing that data.

Management Information System Model

Using the further details described above, we can now draw an MIS model that builds on the organisation's corporate database. In some systems, the separation of basic data-gathering system and MIS would not be so clear cut as depicted here. Instead, they would merely be separate modules of the same overall information system. The data-gathering module would deal largely with data input and storage. The MIS module would deal largely with information retrieval and output.

Benefits of MIS Computerisation

If it functions as anticipated, the creation of a monitoring and control system produces, by definition, greater understanding of the organisation and a greater ability to manage organisational resources and their performance. Within these systems, and by comparison with manual systems, creation of a computerised, rationally-functioning MIS can produce a number of organisational benefits. These include:

— *Faster decision making and control* through provision of timely information. For example, the MIS described by Anthes provided an early warning of performance problems in bulk buying of inputs by US public agencies. Faster decision making released time that would otherwise be tied up on monitoring. Tottle describes the introduction of an MIS to assist government agricultural extension workers in Malaysia. Time was released in this case thanks to upward reporting by the computer system and to exception reporting, which focused the extensionists on those farmers with immediate problems.

— *Better decision making and control:* through provision of relevant information. The Malaysian government workers described by Tottle had a much better understanding of what was going on in their area thanks to the introduction of an MIS. They also had more detailed information which allowed them to provide farmers with a better service, and make better use of available resources. Similarly, in the Anthes example, the statistical analyses gave US state agencies a much better understanding of what was going on in contract bidding. Without the MIS, such an understanding would not have been possible.

In addition, MIS can improve job satisfaction for public servants and can reduce the number of paper records that have to be held.

Examples of Management Information Systems

Management information systems can be introduced to support a variety of public sector applications, as described below.

Transaction-Based MIS

Three main types of management information system fall into this category: accounting, human resources, and 'other'.

Accounting MIS: Far more than anything else, the emphasis of public sector MIS has been on money: on monitoring how much has been spent; on comparing this with budget; and on controlling expenditure to bring it in as close as possible to budget at year-end. Examples of this type of computerisation range from the Kenyan Ministry of Agriculture to major US regulatory agencies.

Typical reports include:

— Statements of account: month-end, year-end, year-to-date, etc.; these will generally have to be designed to fit with existing regulatory or legislative standards for public sector accounting.

— Warnings of budget head over- or under-spend against target; variance from planned budget can be shown either in absolute or in percentage terms.

— Statements of cash requirements in the month ahead based on payments still owed within accounts payable data.

Payroll often represents the main cost for public sector organisations. It has therefore been a starting point for MIS in many organisations, looking to monitor and control salary and income tax payments, and also to issue payments. One focus for payroll MIS in some countries has been to identify and then eliminate 'ghost workers', who do not exist but whose pay is fraudulently collected by other employees. Cain describes the importance of this approach in the creation of MIS for the governments of Ghana, Uganda and Zimbabwe. Examples of payroll reports were described above.

An example of a typical accounting MIS report is shown in Table 1.

Table 1: Accounting MIS Report Example Accounting Report Department of Land Management Year-to-date, end September 1999

Expenditure	*HeadBudget (US$)*	*Actual (US$)*	*Variance*	*(%)*
Salaries	275,900	291,400	15,500	5.6%
Wages	241,200	248,000	6,800	2.8%
Office Equipment	113,600	141,600	28,000	24.6%
Utilities	88,500	84,500	-4,000	-4.5%
Transport	69,300	69,300	0	0%
Consumables	54,900	63,800	8,900	16.2%
Other	127,100	131,100	4,000	3.1%
TOTAL	970,500	1,029,700	59,200	6.1%

The MIS reporting Table 1 has been instructed to highlight all variances greater than US$10,000 and all variances greater than 5 per cent. Rationally, in attempting to control the overspend indicated, management priority would be given to those items highlighted in both columns.

This form of accounting report, based on responsibility for particular budget heads, is widely used in the public sector. Some public sector organisations, especially those providing public services, have developed cost accounting MIS.

These aggregate costs horizontally as they are incurred in the delivery of a service. They therefore require allocation of labour and other costs to particular services during the entire process of providing that service.

This is often difficult but can provide very valuable information in helping to assign a value or cost to a public service, and in comparing costs between public service providers. The British public sector National Health Service, for example, has been creating management information systems that can report health care provision costs down to the level of individual patients. This allows better-informed decisions about prioritising the use of scarce resources. It also allows health units to compare their costs with other units. Income-related MIS are the exception rather than the rule in the public sector. MIS are found, though, reporting on:

— Loans and loan repayment. For example, to report those applicants who have been waiting for more than one month to know if their loan application has been granted.

— Customer payments where cost recovery operates in health, education and other social welfare provision. For example, to report those public hospitals which have recovered most and least per patient treated.

— Customer payments to public sector utilities, transportation, rented housing, and enterprises. In these cases, the MIS are likely to be building upon some form of accounts receivable transaction processing system. For example, to report those customers whose accounts remain outstanding 60 days after bills for provision of utility services were issued.

ii. *Human resources MIS:* Management information systems are used in the entire human resource lifecycle from recruitment to termination or retirement. Reports include:

— *Vacancies*: for example, a detail report on all vacant posts in the organisation.

— *Recruitment and selection*: for example, a summary report on the ethnic origin and sex of all job applicants and recruits for use in equal opportunities monitoring.

— *Staff performance*: for example, an exception report on only those secretarial staff who are able to take shorthand dictation and type at over 50 words per minute.

— *Payroll*: examples have already been given.

— *Training*: for example, an ad hoc report on all those staff who have received training in gender awareness.

— *Staff promotion*: for example, a detail report on all performance assessments for a potentially-promotable member of staff.

— *Staff departure*: for example, a comparative report on turnover rates and reason for departure in the information systems and accounting departments.

— *Pensions*: for example, a summary report on recent annual pension fund growth rates.

— *Other*: for example, a comparative report on workplace accident rates on different days of the week; this and other categories may relate to government reporting and compliance.

The State of Vermont in the US developed a human resources management information system (albeit both over-time and over-budget) that covered a number of these reporting functions. Similar experiences are reported in the development of a personnel information system with MIS capabilities for Northamptonshire County Council, a local government body in the UK.

iii. Other MIS: Public sector inventory information systems tend to be relatively basic and/or automated. The aim of an inventory MIS is to monitor stock levels and to control stocks to ensure that all items are neither over- nor under-stocked.

MIS may also report on other entities such as fixed assets, financial investments and projects. One US regulatory agency, for instance, set up an MIS covering its major facilities in order to monitor, control and then reduce expenditure on those facilities, as requested by Congress.

MIS may also combine the functional areas described above. The British Department of Social Security, for instance, has proceeded with development of an integrated MIS covering financial, personnel and resource management.

Public Administration and Regulation MIS

Management information systems have been created to support the whole range of public administration and regulatory activities. In the US, for example, the National Drivers Register has MIS facilities to report on driver licence details, such as all those within a given state whose licence has been revoked or suspended. Similarly, the US Environmental Protection Agency is pushing forward in use of MIS to help monitor and control environmental risks. Just a couple of other examples are provided here.

i. *Buildings registration MIS:* Based on data recorded about particular types of buildings, or buildings in a particular locality, this could monitor building ownership and use, and produce reports on, for instance:

— all details of one individual building (building code, address, description, owner, floor space, utility connections, local tax liabilities, etc.),

— annual growth in the total number of small industrial units in major cities, or

— all buildings within one city block for which no ownership records were lodged.

Japan's registration MIS has these types of uses in mind. It was begun in earnest in 1988 as a 20-year project, and will eventually cover some 40 million buildings and 230 million parcels of land.

ii. *Taxation MIS:* Based on data recorded about individual tax-paying entities (whether individuals or organisations), this could monitor the payment of taxation, and produce reports on, for instance:

— all details of an individual tax payer (payer code, name, address, employment, employer, tax code, record of assets, record of recent tax payments and liabilities, etc.),

— a summary of sales tax receipts broken down by sector,

— patterns of non-payment in order to target enforcement efforts more effectively, or

— the names and addresses of all those registered on public or private payrolls as tax payers who are also claiming social welfare payments.

The State of New Jersey in the US used the last of these report types to identify welfare cheats and to generate 'estimated savings of $45 million in the first two years of operation'.

Public Service Delivery MIS

Many public service providers have developed management information systems to monitor and control the services that they provide. Both the US and UK Social Security agencies have developed MIS to report on the welfare payments and services that they provide. The British public healthcare system has also been a major investor in MIS as it tries to control healthcare costs and simultaneously improve delivery standards. One further example is provided here.

i. *Education sector MIS for schools:* Based on data gathered from individual schools and from other educational institutions such as exam boards and school inspectorates, this could monitor the provision of education and produce reports on, for instance:

— details of one individual school (school code, name, address, location, staff numbers, student enrolment by year, annual budgets, school facilities, examination grades, etc.),

— a summary of the average staff:student ratio for each state, or

— the name and location of all schools without on-site sports facilities.

An example of a typical school MIS report is shown in Table 2.

Individual schools can also make use of MIS. Hobmoor Junior and Infant School, a public school in Birmingham, UK, introduced a computerised attendance system to produce MIS reports that monitor pupil attendance. This improved the Principal's ability to understand and control absence patterns, resulting in a 2.5 per cent increase in attendance rates.

Management information systems form a bedrock of IT use in the public sector. They are therefore found in all sections of the public sector and in all countries, as the examples cited in this chapter suggest. Of course, different people use the term 'management information system' differently. The term should therefore not form the basis for arguments about what an MIS is and is not. So long as one and those with whom one works understand and agree on a definition, that is good enough. Similarly, when dealing with written material, one needs to be able to understand and communicate, not get locked into doctrinal debate.

On the basis of our definition provided here, though, we can end by summarising a few general points about MIS that differentiate them from other types of public sector information systems:

— Monitoring and control is central; the focus is therefore mainly on information about what has happened (or is happening) rather than, as with planning, what will happen.

— Reports are generally based on relatively simple analysis techniques.

— MIS normally feed into some human decision making, based on their reports; such decision making is usually structured or semi-structured.

— MIS are mainly targeted at operational and tactical management levels.

— Unless custom-written, MIS are often based on a database system, because of the superior query and reporting capabilities of database management systems.

Determining Corruption Impacts

Corruption is a major problem for many parts of the public sector. One dominant vision of corruption restraint – the 'Panoptic vision' – sees information technology (IT) as a key enabler of management control. This chapter presents five short case studies of IT and public sector corruption to test the realities of this Panoptic vision. From these it is concluded that, while IT sometimes does detect and remove corruption, it can also have no effect or even provide new corruption opportunities for some public servants. Management of corruption is ultimately shaped more by management decisions and by broader organisational and environmental factors than it is by technology. Put simply, IT-based systems guided by the Panoptic vision affect symptoms of a corrupt system rather than causes. Public managers must therefore adopt a more holistic vision of corruption control. They must also recognise the link between IT and corruption in the planning of some public sector information systems.

Defining and Controlling Corruption

Corruption – 'inducement to wrong by bribery or other unlawful or improper means' – is a global problem. The focus of this chapter is on corruption within the public sector. In choosing this focus, it must, of course, be recognised that other sectors have corruption problems, and that much of the corruption in state organisations involves payments from the private sector. As an issue, corruption tends to stir strong reactions.

— Corruption is a culture-bound concept: 'Your culture may say that X is corrupt; mine does not'.

— Corruption is a force for good: 'It helps the wheels of government and business to turn'.

— Corruption is too big to deal with: 'Corruption is everywhere. What can we ever hope to do about it?'.

All of these reactions can make it hard for corruption to be addressed by public managers. Yet it is an issue that many of them face, which must be attacked for at least three good reasons:

— It drains off valuable economic resources, particularly investment funds, into unproductive uses, and reduces the likelihood of government objectives being achieved.

— It siphons off another valuable resource – the time of public sector staff – into unproductive use, and creates resentments and frustrations among staff, thus reducing organisational efficiency.

— Because it is hidden and unaccountable, corruption is essentially undemocratic and damages democratic processes and institutions. sustain

One currently-dominant paradigm of corruption control in public administration – termed the 'Panoptic vision' by Anechiarico & Jacobs – sees management techniques of rules and enforcement as the key to controlling corruption. Enforcement is and has always been a labour-intensive and information-intensive activity for which managers require assistance. One model for such assistance is provided by Jeremy Bentham's 19th century idea of the Panopticon: a constructed technology that allowed a single central unseen guard to observe the activity of all prison inmates. In the late 20th century, information technology presents public organisations with the possibility of creating their own Panopticon: one that would allow managers to gaze unseen upon the activities of their employees and thus monitor and control corruption.

But what of reality in public sector organisations: can information technology, in practice, help control corruption? Some thumbnail sketches are offered below to help provide initial pointers to an answer. The cases are drawn from the author's personal field experience and from the direct experiences of public sector managers studying at the University of Manchester.

IT Corruption

Managers in a government-owned railway system were concerned about the efficiency of its seat/berth reservation system, and about corruption within the system. Booking staff had access to and control over the allocation of places on trains. A few would take a bribe (either directly or via a ticket tout) to provide a passenger with a reserved place; these being at a premium since all trains were over-booked. A computerised system was introduced, one objective of which was to eliminate corruption. To achieve this, allocation of reservations was handled automatically, including the particularly 'weak link' of moving passengers on the waiting list into places vacated by cancellations.

Computerisation did make it harder for the clerical staff to be corrupt because the software, not the clerk, now decided – based on booking date – which passengers would fill vacated slots. However, corruption was not eliminated, and two aspects will be noted here.

— Station managers retained manual control over a certain proportion of the train places, supposedly to cover emergencies or last-minute travel by VIPs. Some continued to provide these places to non-emergency, non-VIP passengers in return for cash.

— Ticket touts showed how ingenious and resourceful they can be. Knowing that their best customers were businessmen in a hurry, they would book places well in advance on the main inter-city trains using a very common man's name, citing his age as 35. These places would then be sold at a premium to last minute travellers, most of whom were men who could get away with appearing 35 years old to the ticket collectors.

In a public works department, there was concern about the number of 'ghost workers' in the system. These are people listed on the payroll, and therefore paid, who do not exist in reality. Someone else collects the wages paid out under their name. The payroll system was computerised and, during this process, a check was made between listed and actual workers. Any non-existent staff were removed from the system.

This seemed to have solved the problem, assisted by the word being spread that the computer could make an automatic check between the payroll list and reality, and could automatically detect who was picking up ghost worker wages. Of course, it could do no such thing. An audit 18 months later uncovered a very well-to-do computer operator who was collecting his own wages plus those of thirty other workers he had entered into the payroll system.

Examination marks at a public university were previously kept on paper, with calculation of final grades and averages being done manually by a small group of trusted staff. Mark lists were kept locked in a safe when not being used. Given the large number of students, it was decided to computerise the marks and calculations. There was an assumption that information on the (un-networked) computer would be safe, though a password was added just in case, known only to a very few staff.

All seemed well until one lecturer noticed that a relatively dull student had achieved a spectacular final grade. Enquiries revealed that he was the son of one of the computer managers. The manager, knowing the importance of university grades for job prospects, had opened up the marks database and changed his son's mark. Unfortunately for him, instead of altering the figures slightly, he got over-ambitious and pushed them from the 40s up to the 70s.

Computerisation was taking place in a (different) public university, and it seemed obvious to turn attention to the admissions process, which was notoriously slow and corrupt. Computerisation of admissions involved inputting the school-leaving exam marks of all applicants, and then producing a prioritised list, headed by the candidate with the best overall marks. Other factors might be taken into account but, if all other things are equal and there are 1000 places at the university, the top 1000 candidates on the computer-generated list would be the ones to gain admission.

This clearly represented a considerable threat to members of the admissions committee. These members could gain significant financial and political rewards by offering admission to the stupid sons and daughters of the rich and powerful; children who would not get into university if an entirely merit-based system were adopted. The committee therefore decided to accept the prioritised list merely as an 'advisory tool', and never made it public outside that committee.

A customs department kept manual records with the names and addresses of overseas firms which had been involved in import or export transactions. These contacts were useful to local entrepreneurs, particularly those seeking export collaborations. The entrepreneurs therefore paid customs officials illegally to provide them with the contact details.

The department, including its overseas firm details, was computerised and one computer was put into a front office where members of the public could access it. Entrepreneurs gained direct access to the contact details they wanted and payments were therefore no longer made.

Information about foreign businesses was a resource here which local businesses required. Because the information was scarce and because it was kept as a private resource, customs officials (acting as information 'gatekeepers') were able to charge 'rent' for access to it. Once the information came into the public domain, no access charges could be made.

From the cases, we can conclude that the impacts associated with the introduction of IT in the public sector are quite varied:

— Corruption in an organisation is possible because staff have access to a valued resource and to those who will pay for it. The valued resource could include provision of a service, legal permission to undertake some activity, or information of value. They also have the skills, confidence and autonomy to make decisions about the provision of that resource.

Where IT can deny access to the resource or to relevant decision-making processes, this may remove corruption. Typically this will occur if the processes are automated. For example, the clerical staff in case 1 no longer had control over allocation of vacated reservations. In other cases, computerisation assists detection of corrupt practice, in line with the Panoptic vision. In turn, this reduces staff's perceived autonomy and so is likely to suppress some corrupt practices.

New corruption opportunities

In cases 2 and 3, IT introduction provided new corruption opportunities for some staff that were not previously available. This may often be related to closing down opportunities for other staff. Computerisation does so by creating changes in one or more of four aspects:

— *Skills.* Computerisation is often associated with an 'upskilling' of corruption, providing an opportunity for those with IT skills, and denying those without these skills.

— *Confidence*: Borrowing from the Panoptic vision, a mythical image may be promoted of the computer as an objective, all-seeing, all-knowing machine. This may cause some corrupt staff to lose confidence and to refrain from corrupt practices. Those who understand computers are not put off (and will often spread the mythical image to reduce the likelihood of competition or detection).

— *Access*: In the cases described, computerisation of records was accompanied by closing down access to some staff but opening up access to all those operating the IT systems. With the advent of networked systems, such opportunities for access may greatly increase.

Control: The mask of data quality and computer omnipotence makes some managers assume that IT removes the opportunities for corruption, i.e. that the Panopticon can operate without the need for human intervention. They may therefore fail to institute controls on computerised systems. This assumption provides greater autonomy for IT-literate staff.

The discussions above the computerisation had no effect on corruption. This is because computerised information systems were designed in such a way that key corruption-linked resources or processes were left uncomputerised, despite their possibly being surrounded by other computerisations.

Factors Determining Corruption Impacts

These different impacts can be explained by the different factors involved:

Information technology

Computers have no innate property related to corruption except that of their imagery. They do not automatically provide a Panoptic model of control – this only comes if it is deliberately and systemically designed to do so. The impacts described above therefore principally depend on the design of information systems and of wider organisational systems.

Information system design and management decisions:

The way that computerised information systems are designed significantly determines corruption impacts. This design, in turn, depends on management design decisions. For example, it was a management decision that led to automation of clerical procedures and therefore to the removal of one opportunity for corruption. On the other hand, a management decision was taken to avoid computerising the station managers' allocation of emergency and VIP places.

To some extent, this latter design decision was part of the process of getting computerisation accepted: it was only able to proceed once the decision had been made that computerisation would not threaten these stakeholders' control and private incomes. Indeed, by removing sources of competition for corrupt earnings from the clerical staff, computerisation potentially offered an opportunity for station managers' incomes to be increased.

Other information system components will also affect corruption impacts. For example, the design of work processes will play a role. The presence of IT is largely irrelevant: the department could have made its manual records publicly accessible, leading to a similar result. What mattered was a management decision about the wider re-design of processes that changed the way information flowed in the organisation. Similarly, computerisation had little to do with the removal of ghost workers/claimants and consequent (temporary) removal of corruption. This required the introduction of a process of physical checks, as was done both before and after computerisation.

In all these and other cases, then, it is management decisions about information system design that shape the ultimate impacts. These decisions and designs do not always adhere to the Panoptic vision, with consequent implications for corruption control.

Finally, there are other wider systems components that play a role. For instance, the people involved must have some motivation to act corruptly. In part this depends on fear of detection (which computers may affect), but in the main motivation relates to the wider context, as discussed below. Managers, and others charged with guarding against corruption, must also themselves have the skills, motivation, authority and means to detect and act against corrupt activities. In part, this too depends on wider structures, strategies and culture.

Leaving aside the 'corruption of opportunity', such as that which arose in the payroll case, two particular types of corruption can be distinguished. There is the 'corruption of necessity' practised by poorly-paid, low-level staff. Their incomes do not meet the many demands placed upon them, and they must find ways of supplementation. Computerised information systems may be designed to suppress some of their activities. However, these new IS will not extinguish the underlying motivation for additional income because this arises from a wider context. Thus corruption is almost bound to re-emerge, as it did with the ticket touts. The Panoptic vision is a poor guide to this reality because IT cannot (yet) monitor all activities of all staff.

Alternatively, there is the 'corruption of greed' practised by well-/adequately-paid public servants. These staff may well have senior positions. They have enough income to live on, but want and get more because they are in a position to do so and because it is seen as a natural activity for those in power. Given the power of these staff to determine their working environment, computerised information systems are unlikely to be allowed to have much impact unless imposed by a very strong external agency. Such staff will therefore remain aloof from any Panoptic gaze, exposing a further limitation of the vision as a guide to action.

In all cases, it can be seen that corruption arises from a combination of two sets of factors: the micro-level (the individual, his/her circumstances, needs, skills, access, confidence and autonomy) and the macro-level (organisational and national management systems, politics and culture). As we have seen, management decisions about computerised information systems may affect skills, access, confidence and autonomy. However, they are most unlikely to affect the personal or environmental drivers behind corruption and the Panoptic ideal of corruption controlled by IT is therefore flawed.

To put this in simplified terms, IT-based systems guided by the Panoptic vision affect symptoms of a corrupt system rather than causes. Corruption is a phenomenon rooted in the cultural, political and economic circumstances of those involved. IT does little to affect these root causes, remains limited in its surveillance potential, and so cannot eliminate corruption in the public sector.

Public sector managers therefore require a more holistic vision of corruption control to supersede the Panoptic vision. This would understand the roots of corruption, not just the symptoms. It would address corruption not through individual management techniques but through strategies of institutional and contextual development. It would also see IT as having a potential role, but one which is limited and which forms only one small part of a much larger jigsaw.

Managing IT Introduction in Corrupt Environments

Despite the preceding analysis of IT limitations, experience suggests public servants often perceive that IT introduction is going to have a significant effect of reducing corruption. These perceptions will feed into the process of planning any new information system. The effect of these perceptions is likely to be particularly marked where a new computer system is being introduced in the presence of practices that are currently corrupt. In one government's pensions office, for example, computerisation was roundly resisted. Many factors were at first seen to underlie the resistance including:

— fears of loss of jobs,

— fears that staff would not have the necessary skills,

— health and safety concerns.

What emerged during investigation, however, was that the main fear lay around the issue of corrupt incomes. Pensions staff had the power to deny claimants access to pension payments or to provide claimants with access to certain types of higher-income pension. The staff were using this power to extract bribes from pensionable claimants. They feared that computerisation would remove this power. Hence, their true reason for resistance.

Where resistance and corruption are linked in this way, there are three possible reactions that can be drawn from the case studies above:

— If the computerised system will not have an effect, make this (subtly) clear.

— If the computerised system will affect corruption and the stakeholders are not that powerful, then 'tough it out', i.e. push on in the likelihood that resistance can be overcome.

— If the computerised system will affect corruption and the stakeholders are powerful, change the design plans so that the key corrupt processes are not computerised or are not exposed to monitoring by IT.

'Toughing it out' can also be tried in the last case, and this would seem to be the morally-correct route to take. However, it will greatly increase resistance to IT and the risks of information system failure.

Bibliography

Buss Martin D. J. and Lynn M. Salerno, "Common Sense and Computer Security", *Harvard Business Review*, March-April 1984.

Butler, Gathorne. *Organisation and Management*, Prentice Hall, 1986.

Galliers, R. 'Information systems and technology planning within a competitive strategy framework', in *Information Management. State of the Art Report*, P. Griffiths (ed.), Pergamon, 1986.

Hawkridge David, *New Information Technology in Education*, Croom Helm, London, 1983.

Horowitz Irving Louis, "Printed Words, Computers and Democratic Societies", *The Virginia Quarterly Review*, Autumn 1983.

Huws Ursula, "New Technology Homeworkers," *Employment Gazette*, London, January 1984.

Information Technology and its Impact on American Education, Office of Technology Assessment, US Congress, Washington DC, 1982.

Lynch, Clifford and Preston, Cecelia M. 'Internet access to information resources', *Annual Review of Information Science and Technology*, 25, 1990.

Michel Bauwens, "What Is Cyberspace?", *Computers in Libraries* 14, April, 1994.

Malamud, Carl, *Exploring the Internet: a technical travelogue,* London, Prentice-Hall, 1992.

Mandeville Thomas, "The Spatial Effects of Information Technology", *Futures,* February 1983. A review of the literature on possible urban/regional problems.

Simons G. L., *Privacy in the Computer Age* NCC, Manchester, England, 1982.

_______________ Simons G. L. *Robots in Industry* NCC Publications, Manchester, England, 1981.

Smith, Christine H. (ed.), *Open Systems Interconnection: the Communications Technology of the 1990s,* London, KG Saur, 1988.

Tranfield, David. 'Management information systems: an exploration of core philosophies', *Journal of Applied Systems Analysis,* vol. 10, 1983.

Treleaven Philip C. and Isabel Gouveia Lima, "Japan's Fifth Generation Computer Systems", *Computer,* August 1982.

Trist, Eric, *et al. Organisational Choice,* Tavistock, 1963.

Waltz David L., "Artificial Intelligence," *Scientific American,* October 1982.

Index